Andrew Foyle is a solicitor advocate and the Head of Litigation for Scotland at Shoosmiths LLP, with over 17 year's experience advising and representing financial institutions and insolvency practitioners at all levels of the Court system in Scotland. His experience in the financial sector involves both pursuing and defending claims, including secured and unsecured asset/credit recovery, regulatory issues, mis-selling claims, fraud, negligence and contractual claims. He has been involved in a number of recent high profile cases in the banking sphere and has spent periods on secondment with two major clearing banks.

A Practical Guide to the Law of Prescription in Scotland

A Practical Guide to the Law of Prescription in Scotland

Andrew Foyle
LL.B. (Hons), LL.M., Dip LP, NP,
Solicitor Advocate
Partner in Commercial Litigation at Shoosmiths LLP, Edinburgh

Law Brief Publishing

Published 2020 by Law Brief Publishing, an imprint of Law Brief Publishing Ltd
30 The Parks
Minehead
Somerset
TA24 8BT

www.lawbriefpublishing.com

Paperback: 978-1-912687-64-0

To Kirsty, Daniel and Dermot.

PREFACE

There have been a number of momentous changes to the law of prescription since the last major work in this area was published. The Supreme Court rulings in *Morrison* and *Gordon's Trustees* (both examined at Chapter 5) and the forthcoming changes in the Prescription (Scotland) Act 2018 (examined in Chapter 8) have fundamentally altered an area of law which had been broadly unchanged for over 40 years.

However, this is not intended to be an academic work. Rather the aim is to look at the law from the standpoint of the civil litigation practitioner and to consider what such a practitioner ought to know before putting pen to paper in order to draft their writ or summons. For that reason it does not examine in any depth areas of the law which, whilst perhaps interesting, are rarely seen in practice. It focusses instead on questions which have arisen in my own practice and that of my colleagues, and on the answers which I have arrived at through 18 years of civil litigation experience.

There are many people I should thank.

Firstly, my wife and children for putting up with me, both in general and also whilst I locked myself away in order to write this.

Secondly, my team at Shoosmiths with whom I have had many lively discussions on the topic (one of which resulted in the phrase "Schrodinger's Prescription", of which I am rather too proud, and which you'll find reference to at Chapter 4). The debates within our group helped enormously in focussing my thinking on certain topics within this book.

Thirdly, all of those who have attended seminars I have given on this topic in the past. There are too many to name (and it would be a GDPR nightmare in any event), but your inciteful questions over the years have helped me to focus this work on what is genuinely seen in practice.

And finally to Tim and Garry at Law Brief Publishing, for asking me to write this and for the support and helpful feedback as the drafting has progressed.

Of course, any errors which remain in this book are entirely my own. The law is stated as it stands on 1st December 2019.

Andrew Foyle
December 2019

CONTENTS

CHAPTER ONE
INTRODUCTION – WHAT IS PRESCRIPTION?

What Is Prescription and Why Do We Have It?

The subject matter of this book is the law of prescription in Scotland. In particular it is concerned with "negative prescription", i.e. the loss of rights or extinction of obligations over time. That is to be contrasted with "positive prescription" – the acquisition of rights after a period of time, particularly in relation to heritable property. An exposition of positive prescription, whilst interesting, is outwith the scope of this book.

The intention is to offer an understanding to the practitioner of the operation of prescription and matters to consider when a practitioner approaches a potential claim. But let us start from the beginning: what is prescription and how does it differ from other forms of time bar?

Most legal systems contain a mechanism whereby claims can no longer be pursued through the courts after the passage of a specified amount of time. In most jurisdictions those periods can vary from claim to claim.

In French law[1], for example, most claims require to be brought within 5 years, although claims arising from rights over heritable property are generally subject to a 30-year time bar period. Our nearest neighbours, England & Wales also have variable time limits, with the general rule for most civil claims being 6 years, but some claims such as actions under deed or enforcement of mortgages being prestable for up to 12 years.[2]

1 Loi No. 2208-561 of 17 June 2008

2 See the Limitation Act 1980, part I

Scotland is therefore no different from most of our European neighbours in having periods after which a claim may not be brought to court. Unlike some, however (and including our compatriots south of the border), when our time bar limit is reached, the claim is entirely extinguished. In England the period is a limitation period, meaning it can't be pursued through the courts, but – for example in debt cases – a party is still (subject to regulatory constraints[3]) at liberty to demand payment or report the matter to a credit reference agency. We return to this difference below.

One fundamental question is why legal systems need a time bar rule. It is obvious that such a rule might operate unfavourably on a claimant who would have an otherwise valid claim against his or her debtor. By definition it allows for the possibility of a person subject to a perfectly legitimate claim "to get away with it" if they simply sit tight for the requisite amount of time.

This is all true, of course, but there is a counter argument that having a sword of Damocles hanging over one's head for an indeterminate period of time is equally unfair. As it was put by the Scottish Law Commission in their 1970 Report:

> "*The law should not give countenance to latent and antiquated claims which may affect even the successors of the person responsible and, if revived after many years, may disturb the basis upon which they have arranged their lives.*"[4]

So, what a legal system is trying to achieve in setting its time-bar periods is a balance between a reasonable amount of time to get one's case in order and pursue a claim, without the need for a potential defender to put their life on hold for an unreasonable interval whilst a pursuer gets organised.

3 See, e.g., The FCA's Handbook, CONC 7.15

4 Scot Law Com No. 15, Reform of the Law Relating to Prescription and Limitation of Actions, at Para 34(2)

The law in this area in Scotland goes back a very long way. Prior to examination by the Scottish Law Commission in 1970, the law of prescription remained governed by the Prescription Act 1474 and the Prescription Act 1617. The law had been amended and interpreted in numerous ways over the years but much of it was still written in old Scots.

Nevertheless, the Scottish Law Commission's primary intention in 1970 was not to re-write the law of prescription – it was not seen as being broken – and nor was it intended that what became the Prescription & Limitation (Scotland) Act 1973 should be a radical departure from the pre-existing law. Rather the aim was that the whole of the law and practice should be brought within one Act and amended only insofar as common sense and clarity required. This explains why we have some particularly archaic wording and concepts in the Act, many of which are rarely, if ever, relied upon.

The outcome of the 1970 report was the Prescription & Limitation (Scotland) Act 1973 (hereinafter "the 1973 Act"). The 1973 Act, whilst not perfect, was undoubtedly an improvement on the ancient and obscure legislation which had gone before.

In 1983 the Commission looked again at this area of law, this time with a focus on personal injuries and aspects of private international law which were beginning to impinge upon Scotland.

As the 1983 Report makes clear, the law was not in disarray. The Commission point out that:

> *"Commentators on the consultative memorandum for the most part expressed satisfaction with the law, though not with its presentation. There is now wide acceptance of a short limitation period, running from the date of injury, but sufficiently flexible to take account of the claimant's lack of knowledge of such matters as the existence and cause of his injury. We have therefore seen our main task as one of*

simplifying the law and eradicating a number of obvious defects, and this is something which we believe can be readily achieved."[5]

The 1983 Report therefore recommended only minor changes, most notably imposing the short negative prescription to personal injury cases, where previously the 20-year period had applied. It also proposed to introduce a limitation period of three years for certain types of claim.

How Does Prescription Differ From Limitation?

As we have seen above, Scots law now has both prescriptive periods and, in relation to specific types of claim, limitation periods. Other jurisdictions only have limitation periods.

It is beyond the scope of this book to examine limitation in Scotland, but it is important to understand the difference between the two, particularly when considering the consequences of a claim having prescribed.

The difference is relatively straightforward. A limitation period imposes a time limit after which a claim may not be litigated – that is 3 years for most personal injury claims not resulting in death. The claim itself, however, still exists. In terms of Section 19A of the 1973 Act, the court has the power (although it is used sparingly) to waive the three-year period and to allow a claim to proceed.

Limitation can be contrasted with prescription, therefore. Prescription is where the claim itself is wholly extinguished and cannot be pursued by any means whatsoever – it simply no longer exists. If a claim has prescribed, the court has no power to waive the period. The consequences flowing from the existence of a claim, for example reports to credit reference agencies in the case of consumer debt, must likewise be considered to have fallen.

---

5 Scot Law Com No. 74, Report on Prescription and the Limitation of Actions, etc., at para 1.4

If a claim is to survive the prescriptive period it must fall within an exception to the general rule, whether through the period having been interrupted or suspended. This is discussed in more detail below.

Fundamental Concepts of Prescription

As a legal concept, prescription appears to be straightforward in principle: after a period of time a claim no longer exists. However there are a number of matters to be aware of when considering whether a claim has prescribed and numerous grey areas where the law is less clear than one would expect given its lengthy pedigree.

The period of time after which a claim prescribes is generally referred to as the "prescriptive period" and that terminology will be used throughout the rest of this work. The general principle is that a claim or obligation will expire following upon a period of 20 years without the obligation being insisted upon, unless it is either (a) subject to a different prescriptive period, usually of five years (although see below); (b) listed in the Act as being imprescriptible; or (c) subject to an interruption.

The length of the prescriptive period depends upon the nature of the obligation. For most purposes that period will be either five years or 20 years, however it is important to note the different periods contained in the 1973 Act for specific types of claim.[6] We return to these, briefly, below.

It is also important to note that (for the time being) not all of the answers will be found in the four corners of the 1973 Act. There are a number of claims and obligations where other statutes set out different prescriptive or limitation periods which override the 1973 Act. Examples include claims for loss of goods at sea, where the period is one

6 i.e. the two-year period for claims for contributions between wrongdoers (Section 8A) and the ten-year period for damages arising from product liability claims (Section 22A)

year,[7] or claims for delivery up of goods infringing copyright under the Copyright Designs & Patents Act 1988, which has a six year limitation period.[8] A number of time limits are also set in planning legislation and in claims before employment tribunals. A detailed examination of these areas is beyond the scope of this book, but a prudent legal practitioner should be aware of any limits set out in governing legislation at the outset of considering any claim that they may be taking on behalf of a client.

Turning back to the 1973 Act, it is submitted that the key to understanding the law of prescription comes from understanding:

- which prescriptive period applies to which obligations in terms of the Act;
- when the prescriptive period begins to run in each case; and
- what events can interrupt the prescriptive period, either starting it anew or suspending it temporarily.

The 1973 Act deals with all of these rules within a few short sections. We shall now examine those provisions in more detail.

7 Carriage of Goods by Sea Act 1971

8 Sections 113 and 203

CHAPTER TWO
WHAT ARE THE PRESCRIPTIVE PERIODS?

There are four negative prescription periods set out in the 1973 Act. Those are the periods of 20 years and five years, which are examined in more detail below; a period of ten years in relation to claims made under Section 2 of the Consumer Protection Act 1987[1]; and a period of two years in relation to contributions between wrongdoers.[2]

In addition to these periods, and whilst it is outwith the scope of this book to examine the concept of Limitation of actions under Part II of the 1973 Act, it is important to be aware of the limitation periods applicable to actions for recovery under proceeds of crime legislation as they would be easy to overlook.

The Ten-Year Period

Claims under Part I of the Consumer Protection Act 1987 relate to reparation for damage caused wholly or partly as a result of a defect in a product. In addition to the ten-year prescriptive period, such claims are also subject to a three-year limitation period.[3]

The ten-year period is intended as a long-stop date. Accordingly, unlike the other prescriptive periods, it is not interrupted by a relevant acknowledgement. Moreover, a relevant claim under Section 22A will not commence a new period, but merely delay the end of the prescriptive period until final disposal of the claim.[4]

---

1 See Section 22A of the 1973 Act

2 Section 8A of the 1973 Act

3 Section 22B of the 1973 Act

4 Section 22A(2) of the 1973 Act

The Two-Year Period

Section 8A of the 1973 Act introduces a two-year prescriptive period in relation to any obligation to make a contribution by virtue of Section 3(2) of the Law Reform (Miscellaneous Provisions)(Scotland) Act 1940 in respect of any damages or expenses.

The 1940 Act applies where in an action of damages for loss or damage arising from any wrongful acts or negligent acts or omissions two or more people are found to be jointly and severally liable by the court or jury. If one such person pays any damages or expenses for which they are found liable, they are entitled to recover from any other person who, if they had been sued, would have been found liable.

In terms of Section 8A of the 1973 Act, such a claim must be brought within two years, failing which it shall be extinguished. This prescriptive period can be interrupted by a relevant claim or a relevant acknowledgement and is subject to the same interruptions as the five-year period under Section 6.

Proceeds of Crime / Criminal Activity

Whilst technically a limitation period rather than a prescriptive period, it is important to be aware of the constraints incumbent upon the Scottish Ministers in relation to actions for civil recovery under certain legislation.

Under section 19B of the 1973 Act proceedings for a Recovery Order in respect of any recoverable property under the Proceeds of Crime Act 2002 must be commenced within a period of 20 years from the date upon which the right of action accrued. In the case of property obtained through unlawful conduct, the right of action is taken to have accrued on the date the property is obtained. In the case of any other recoverable property, that date will be the date upon which property obtained by the unlawful conduct it represents is obtained.

This rule also applies to proceedings under Section 13(5) of the Criminal Finances Act 2017. That provision concerns property obtained through unlawful conduct relating to gross abuses of human rights. The period would run from the date upon which the conduct constituting the abuse of human rights occurs.[5]

There is also a 20-year rule in relation to proceedings under the Proceeds of Crime Act 2002 (External Requests and Orders) Order 2005.[6] Again, the period begins to run from the date upon which the property was obtained as a result of criminal conduct. If that date is not known, then it runs from the date when it is believed to have been obtained. Proceedings for realisation of property pursuant to an external Order under the 2005 Order must also be commenced within 20 years of the date when the property was obtained.[7]

Proceedings for exploitation proceeds orders under the Coroners and Justice Act 2009 must be brought within five years of the date from which the enforcement authority has actual knowledge that exploitation proceeds have been obtained.[8]

These periods are limitation periods. As such, proceedings may not be brought but the obligation might still be said to subsist, and it is potentially open to the relevant authorities to take steps other than applications to the court.

The remainder of this book will focus on the 20-year and five-year periods, which are the most commonly applied periods, encompassing the vast majority of obligations.

---

5 1973 Act, Section 19B(4A)

6 1973 Act, Section 19BA

7 1973 Act, Section 19C

8 1973 Act, Section 19D

The 20-Year Period

Whilst we have seen that there are exceptions, in most cases which come to the attention of the courts one of two prescriptive periods will usually apply – the 20-year period (known as the "long negative prescription") and the five-year period (known as the "short negative prescription").

It is most convenient to introduce the concept of the differing prescriptive periods by beginning with the long negative prescription. That period, as we shall see, is both a prescriptive period in its own right in relation to certain obligations, and also the "long stop" period which is intended to apply in almost all cases. As we shall also see, it's effectiveness as a back stop is open to question as the law currently stands. That position will change, however, once the Prescription (Scotland) Act 2018 comes into force.

Long negative prescription is introduced by Section 7 of the 1973 Act, which states that:

> "*If, after the date when any obligation to which this section applies has become enforceable, the obligation has subsisted for a continuous period of twenty years—*
>
> *(a) without any relevant claim having been made in relation to the obligation, and*
>
> *(b) without the subsistence of the obligation having been relevantly acknowledged,*
>
> *then as from the expiration of that period the obligation shall be extinguished*"[9]

9 Section 7(1)

Section 7(2) provides that the section applies to an obligation of any kind, including an obligation to which the five-year period applies. However, it does not apply where the obligation is (a) imprescriptible[10], (b) subject to the ten-year period set out above, or (c) subject to the provisions of Part II of the Act (reparations for personal injuries or in respect of death due to personal injury).

Whilst Section 7 applies to obligations, Section 8 of the Act makes clear that a 20-year period also applies to rights, and in particular those relating to heritable and moveable property (subject to judicial interruption). In the event that such a right lies unexercised or unenforced for a period of 20 years, it shall be extinguished unless it is an imprescriptible right under Schedule 3. This provision does not apply to rights which are correlative to an obligation to which Section 6 or 7 of the 1973 Act apply. Such rights accordingly fall with the obligation.

In most cases, one is concerned with the enforcement of obligations rather than rights. In those cases, broadly speaking, the 20-year period will apply in every case because even where the five-year period applies, the 20-year period will also apply[11] as the long-stop date after which all prescriptible claims should expire.

As has been recognised by the Scottish Law Commission in their 2017 Report on Prescription,[12] however, the "long stop" function of the 20-year period does not always operate as such. For one thing, the 20-year period can be interrupted in the same way as the five-year period: through a relevant claim being made or through a relevant acknowledgement.[13] Such an interruption would have the effect of starting a new period. In theory a claim might become imprescriptible through

10 Imprescriptible obligations are set out in Schedule 3 of the 1973 Act

11 Section 7(2) of the 1973 Act

12 Scot Law Com No 247, para 4.15

13 Section 7(1) of the 1973 Act

continual interruption. As we shall come to below, it is intended that the new Prescription (Scotland) Act 2018 will address this anomaly.

The Five-Year Period

Having established that the 20-year period applies in almost every case as the theoretical long stop date after which all obligations (save those which are imprescriptible) ought to expire, the next point to consider is whether the five-year period applies.

The starting point for identifying whether the five-year period applies is Section 6(1) of the 1973 Act, which provides that:-

> "*If, after the appropriate date, an obligation to which this section applies has subsisted for a continuous period of five years—*
>
> *(a) without any relevant claim having been made in relation to the obligation, and*
>
> *(b) without the subsistence of the obligation having been relevantly acknowledged,*
>
> *then as from the expiration of that period the obligation shall be extinguished:*"

Section 6(2) goes on to state that Schedule 1 of the 1973 Act shall have effect for the purpose of defining the obligations to which Section 6 applies. The obligations set out in Schedule 1, to which the five-year period applies are:

(1) Any obligation to pay a sum of money due in respect of a particular period[14]—

(i) by way of interest;

14 1973 Act, Schedule 1, para 1(a)

(ii) by way of an instalment of an annuity;

(iii) by way of rent or other periodical payment under a lease;

(iv) by way of a periodical payment in respect of the occupancy or use of land, not being an obligation falling within any other provision;

(v) by way of a periodical payment under a title condition, not being an obligation falling within any other provision;

(2) Any obligation to pay compensation to a landlord arising from the abolition of leasehold casualties by virtue of section 2 of the Leasehold Casualties (Scotland) Act 2001.[15] As that provision required the landlord to make a claim not later than one year after the date upon which the Act received Royal Assent, such claims are virtually unknown in current practice.

(3) Any obligation to make a compensatory payment to a former superior under the Abolition of Feudal Tenure etc. (Scotland) Act 2000 in respect of the abolition of feuduty.[16] Again, that Act required former superiors to give notice to their former vassal within two years of the appointed day and so such claims are almost unknown in modern practice.

(4) Any obligation arising by virtue of a right–

(i) of reversion under the third proviso to section 2 of the School Sites Act 1841 (or of reversion under that proviso as applied by virtue of any other enactment);

---

15 1973 Act, Schedule 1, para 1(aa)

16 1973 Act, Schedule 1, para 1 (aa) – the numbering of this provision may be a drafting error as it is the same as the preceding provision.

(ii) to petition for a declaration of forfeiture under section 7 of the Entail Sites Act 1840[17]

(5) Any obligation to pay a sum of money by way of costs to which section 12 of the Tenements (Scotland) Act 2004 applies.[18] That provision applies to the liabilities of former owners of a property and the new owners in relation to any outstanding relevant costs, such as property maintenance charges and provides that each are severally liable for such costs in certain circumstances.

(6) Any obligation to make a payment of compensation or any additional payments by a former tenant to a former landlord in relation to the abolition of long leases under section 46, 53(2) or 54(5) of the Long Leases (Scotland) Act 2012.[19]

(7) Any obligation to pay compensation by virtue of section 84 (compensation by the Keeper of the Register of Scotland for certain expenses and losses relating to rectification of the register) [20] or Section 111 (compensation payable to the Keeper relating to a failure to take reasonable care to prevent inaccuracies in the Register)[21] of the Land Registration etc. (Scotland) Act 2012.

(8) Any obligation arising by virtue of a right to redress under Part 4A of the Consumer Protection from Unfair Trading Regulations 2008 (SI 2008/1277).[22]

17 1973 Act, Schedule 1, para 1(ab)

18 1973 Act, Schedule 1, para 1(ac)

19 1973 Act, Schedule 1, para 1(aca)

20 1973 Act, Schedule 1, para 1(ad)

21 1973 Act, Schedule 1, para 1(ae)

22 1973 Act, Schedule 1, para 1(af)

(9) Any obligation based on redress of unjustified enrichment, including without prejudice to that generality any obligation of restitution, repetition or recompense.[23]

(10) Any obligation to make payment to the Scottish Ministers under Section 63 of the Social Security (Scotland) Act 2018.[24] That provision deals with an individual's liability to make payment to the Ministers of the value of any assistance given to the individual due to an error. Where the assistance was given in a form other than money, the obligation will be for the monetary cost of the assistance to the Ministers.[25]

(11) Any obligation arising from *negotiorum gestio*[26]. *Negotiorium gestio* is not a concept commonly encountered in modern times. It appears to be a form of agency where a person intervenes to take on another's affairs without holding formal authority to do so when that person is unable to manage them themselves. It requires to be reasonable to assume that authority would have been given if the principal had been capable of giving consent. The provision covers any obligation so arising, and so will include both claims by the agent or claims against him by the principal. There appear to be no recent cases involving the concept.

(12) Any obligation arising from liability (whether arising from any enactment or from any rule of law) to make reparation.[27]

---

23 1973 Act, Schedule 1, para 1(b)

24 1973 Act, Schedule 1, para 1(ba)

25 Social Security (Scotland) Act 2018, Section 63(3)

26 1973 Act, Schedule 1, para 1(c)

27 1973 Act, Schedule 1, para 1(d)

(13) Any obligation arising by virtue of section 7A(1) of the Criminal Injuries Compensation Act 1995.[28] This relates to claims by the Scottish Ministers for recovery from offenders of sums paid over to victims in respect of compensation for criminal injury.[29]

(14) Any obligation under a bill of exchange or a promissory note.[30]

(15) Any obligation of accounting, other than accounting for trust funds.[31]

(16) Any obligation arising from, or by reason of any breach of, a contract or promise which does not fall within any other provision.[32] A promise, in law, is to be distinguished from an offer. The former is a unilateral obligation recognised by the law of Scotland and is subject to the short negative prescription; the latter is not and may lapse after a reasonable period of time.[33]

Whilst many of those claims listed in paragraph 1 of Schedule 1 are self-explanatory, much of Schedule 1 is ambiguous. In some marginal cases – as referred to further below – the difference between a claim having prescribed or not can often be down to the way an action is pled.

---

28 1973 Act, Schedule 1, para 1(dd)

29 Whilst outside the scope of this book, it appears that Section 7A was inserted into the 1995 Act by the Management of Offenders, etc. (Scotland) Act 2005. However the 2005 Act achieves this by reference to provisions in the Domestic Violence, Crime and Victims Act 2004 which do not appear to have come into force. It may be questioned, therefore, whether Section 7A of the 1995 Act is properly enacted.

30 1973 Act, Schedule 1, para 1(e)

31 1973 Act, Schedule 1, para 1(f)

32 1973 Act, Schedule 1, para 1(g)

33 See W.W. McBryde, *The Law of Contract in Scotland* (3rd Ed., W. Green, 2007), at Para 6-52

After setting out those claims to which the five-year period applies, paragraph 2 of Schedule 1 then goes on to set out a number of obligations to which the Schedule does not apply. Those obligations are:-

(1) Any obligation to recognise or obtemper a decree of court, an arbitration award or an order of a tribunal or authority exercising jurisdiction under any enactment. A court decree is accordingly enforceable for at least a 20-year period, although given that execution of diligence represents a relevant claim[34], that period can be extended far beyond 20 years through enforcement of the decree.

(2) Any obligation arising from the issue of a bank note.

(3) Any obligation under a contract of partnership or of agency, not being an obligation remaining, or becoming, prestable on or after the termination of the relationship between the parties under the contract. Put another way, claims against fellow partners arising during the currency of the partnership are excepted from the 5-year rule. Those arising on termination of the partnership or after it has ended are not.

(4) Any obligation relating to land, including an obligation to recognise a servitude and any obligation of the Keeper of the Registers of Scotland to pay compensation by virtue of section 77 or 94 of the Land Registration etc. (Scotland) Act 2012. Section 77 concerns claims under the Keeper's warranty. Section 94 relates to compensation payable by the Keeper to persons deprived of a right under Part 9 of the Act or proprietors of property burdened by a servitude created under Section 90.

(5) Any obligation to satisfy a claim to *legitim*, *jus relicti* or *jus relictae*, or to any prior right of a surviving spouse under section 8

34 1973 Act, Section 9(1)

or 9 of the Succession (Scotland) Act 1964. This provision is of some importance. Some estates can take a significant period to wind up. In many cases executries can be administered for more than 5 years. This provision means that rights of certain beneficiaries prescribe after 20 years.

(6) Any obligation to make reparation in respect of personal injuries within the meaning of Part II of the 1973 Act or in respect of the death of any person as a result of such injuries. This is, of course, subject to separate rules contained in Part II, including a limitation period.

(7) Any obligation to make reparation or otherwise make good in respect of defamation within the meaning of section 18A of the 1973 Act. Section 18A provides for a 3-year limitation period for such claims.

(8) Any obligation arising from liability under section 2 of the Consumer Protection Act 1987 to make reparation for damage caused wholly or partly by a defect in a product. This is subject to the 10-year period described above.

(9) Any obligation specified in Schedule 3 to this Act as an imprescriptible obligation.

The provisions of Schedule 1 are exhaustive. If an obligation does not fit within one of the sub-paragraphs of Paragraph 1 (as clarified by paragraph 2), the five-year period does not apply and so the 20-year period will instead apply, unless the obligation is imprescriptible.

We now turn to those obligations which are imprescriptible.

Imprescriptable Rights and Obligations

Schedule 3 of the 1973 Act governs those rights and obligations which do not prescribe. The obligations in question are (following the lettering and numbering used in Schedule 3):

(a) Any real right of ownership in land. This right is reasonably self-explanatory, but must of course be contrasted with a personal or contractual right to obtain title to land, which would not fall within the provision.

(b) The right in land of the lessee under a recorded lease. A lease may only be recorded if for a term of 20 years or longer.[35] The effect of recording the lease is to confer real rights on the tenant. The use of the word "recorded" appears to date back to the pre-Land Registration era, where deeds were recorded in the Register of Sasines. In modern practice titles are now "registered" in the Land Register rather than "recorded". Other sections of the 1973 Act make the distinction.[36] It does not appear, however, that this provision has ever been commented upon judicially. There is no reason in principle why Sasine titles would be treated differently from Land Register titles and it is submitted that the omission of the word "registered" is (or ought to be) of little consequence in practice.

(c) Any right exercisable as a *res merae facultatis*; This is an obscure term, no doubt carried over from the archaic pre-1973 law. Commentators have struggled to define it[37], and there is some conflicting authority. In broad terms it refers to a right which can be exercised at will by the person that holds it. There is no recent authority from which examples can be gleaned, and

35 Land Tenure Reform (Scotland) Act 1974, Sections 8 - 10

36 See, e.g., Section 2 (as amended by the Land Registration etc. (Scotland) Act 2012)

37 The most complete modern attempt to explain the concept is D. Johnston, *Prescription & Limitation* (2nd Edition), W. Green, 2012, at para 3.07 *et seq.*

claims based on this right appear to be virtually unknown in modern practice.

(d) Any right to recover property *extra commercium*. Again, this term is archaic and difficult to define. It appears that a *res extra commercium* is something which is not capable of private ownership. As with *res merae facultatis* modern examples are virtually unknown and are unlikely to be seen in practice.

(e) Any obligation of a trustee—

i. to produce accounts of the trustee's intromissions with any property of the trust;
ii. to make reparation or restitution in respect of any fraudulent breach of trust to which the trustee was a party or was privy;
iii. to make furthcoming to any person entitled thereto any trust property, or the proceeds of any such property, in the possession of the trustee, or to make good the value of any such property previously received by the trustee and appropriated to his own use;

(f) Any obligation of a third party to make furthcoming to any person entitled thereto any trust property received by the third party otherwise than in good faith and in his possession. The distinction between trust property acquired in good faith and property not acquired in good faith is to be noted. If the property is acquired in good faith, any obligation to make it over to the true owner shall prescribe.

(g) Any right to recover stolen property from the person by whom it was stolen or from any person privy to the stealing thereof. The phrase "privy to the stealing thereof" is important. It is often said that good title cannot pass on stolen goods in

Scotland, and that is correct.[38] However the right to recover that property from a *bona fide* third party does prescribe, and the clock will start to tick on such a claim from the point at which they acquire the property in good faith.

(h) Any right to be served as heir to an ancestor or to take any steps necessary for making up or completing title to any real right in land. The first part of this provision refers to a procedure known to the law prior to 1964, and which was replaced by the Succession (Scotland) Act 1964. As such it seems unlikely that examples will be seen in modern practice. It is to be assumed that the second part of the provision is to be taken in the same context as the first – i.e. that this provision deals with questions of succession. The second part of this provision is therefore of some importance, and means that the right of an heir to complete title to any real right in land will not prescribe. As set out above, it would appear that other than this provision, any other right (short of a real right) in property will be subject to negative prescription.

(i) Any obligation of the Keeper of the Registers of Scotland to rectify an inaccuracy in the Land Register of Scotland.[39] It is to be noted that whilst the Keeper's obligation to rectify the Register does not prescribe, we have already seen that the right to claim compensation consequent to such a rectification is subject to the five-year negative prescriptive period.[40]

---

38 This is usually referred to by its latin maxim *nemo dat quod non habet* (nobody can pass better title than they themselves have).

39 See Part 8 of the Land Registration etc. (Scotland) Act 2012.

40 1973 Act, Schedule 1, para 1(ad) and 1(ae)

Grey Areas

In many cases the identification of the correct prescriptive period is straightforward. As can clearly be seen from case law, however, there are grey areas. In some cases the skill of the drafter of pleadings can prove decisive, although the courts have clarified a number of areas.

In *Miller –v- Glasgow District Council,*[41] for example, the issue was the interpretation of "obligation to make reparation" in terms of Schedule 1 of the 1973 Act. The Pursuer in this case sought to compel her local authority to carry out reinstatement works following damage caused to her property through the Council's fault. The question arose as to whether what was being sought could be classified as "reparation" under Schedule 1. If it was, it was common ground that the claim would have prescribed.

> "*The first matter to consider is the generally accepted meaning of the word 'reparation' in the law of Scotland. From the authorities to which we were referred it is apparent that the word is used in the sense of* reparatio injuriarum, *and is a pecuniary remedy which the law of Scotland affords for a loss caused by a wrong.*"[42]

The remedy sought by the pursuer in this case was *ad factum praestandum*[43] and not pecuniary in nature. It therefore did not fall within the schedule as it was not properly "reparation". As a result, the 20-year period applied and the obligation had not prescribed.

Reparation was also considered in another case[44] where damages were sought by a party in relation to an enforcement notice under planning legislation, which was subsequently overturned. The pursuer referred the claim to the Lands Tribunal around 8 years later (albeit he had

41 1988 SC 440

42 *per* Lord Grieve, at p.444

43 i.e. for the performance of a specific act.

44 *Holt –v- Dundee DC* 1990 SLT (Lands Tr) 30

complied with other deadlines within the legislation). It was argued that the claim was one for reparation and that it had prescribed.

It was held that a liability to pay damages by way of statutory compensation under planning legislation was not an obligation to make reparation within para.1(d), and that the five year prescriptive period in s.6(1) of the Prescription and Limitation (Scotland) Act 1973 did not apply to claims under the legislation, the only applicable time bars being those in the planning legislation itself.

The question of what is an "obligation relating to land" has also exercised the courts over the years. In *Lord Advocate –v- Shipbreaking Industries Ltd*[45] The defender leased certain premises from the Ministry of Defence. The lease was a registrable lease and contained provisions for the payment of compensation for damage arising from the defender's occupation upon termination of the lease.

The lease was terminated in 1981. In 1987 the Lord Advocate raised proceedings for compensation arising from the lease. The defender argued that the claim had prescribed as more than five years had elapsed since termination.

The issue before the court was whether the obligation, being contained within a registrable lease, was in fact an obligation relating to land and therefore taken out of the scope of the five-year prescriptive period by paragraph 2 of schedule 1. The court held that it was not:-

> *"[it] seems to me that, on a straightforward reading of the words, an obligation to make reparation for breach of an obligation to do something on land is not itself an obligation relating to land. Counsel for the pursuer did not concede that on his construction of the subparagraph it would follow that any contract to do work on land would have to be treated as one relating to the land. It seems to me, however, that that consequence must follow and accordingly that, as*

45 1991 SLT 838

counsel for the defenders submitted, the effect of the pursuer's argument would be to except a wide variety of obligations from the five year prescriptive period."[46]

An obligation relating to land does not, therefore include an obligation to carry out works on land. That makes logical sense, as otherwise the provision would be apt to cover (for example) tradesmen's accounts.

In another case the court was asked to consider whether a unilateral undertaking or promise in relation to the transfer of land might be considered an obligation relating to land.[47]

In that case the pursuer sought a declarator that her brother had given an undertaking in relation to the transfer of land. The undertaking was given more than 5 years prior to the raising of the action. The question arose as to whether the obligation had prescribed.

The pursuer argued that it was an obligation relating to land, and therefore taken out of the scope of Section 6 by paragraph 2 of Schedule 1 of the 1973 Act. The defender argued that the five-year prescriptive period applied.

It was held that undertaking was not an obligation relating to land in terms of Sch.1 para.2(e) but was rather "an obligation arising from, or by reason of any breach of, a contract or promise" in terms of Sch.1 para.1(g). The obligation accordingly fell squarely within Section 6 and had thus prescribed.

The case of *Cumbernauld Housing Partnership –v- Davies*[48] deals with a number of issues arising from liability for factoring charges payable under a deed of conditions registered in the Land Register. In this case the Sheriff Principal granted Decree against the defender for payment of

46 *per* Lord Coulsfield at p. 839

47 *Smith –v- Stuart* 2004 SLT (Sh Ct) 2

48 2015 SC 532

property factoring fees and costs. The defender appealed to the Inner House on a number of grounds.

The questions before the court included: (a) were the charges "obligations relating to land", so that the five-year period did not apply; and (b) if they were not obligations relating to land, did the registration of a notice of potential liability under the Tenements (Scotland) Act 2004 render it as such an obligation.

It was held that the defender's liability for a share of maintenance costs imposed by her title conditions was a liability by virtue of a management scheme in terms of s.11(9) of the 2004 Act and therefore a relevant cost in terms of s.12 thereof. As such, the obligation to pay a share of factoring costs was subject to extinction by operation of the five-year negative prescription.

In relation to the second point, the registration of notices of potential liability for the costs of common repair work in terms of sections 12 and 13 of the 2004 Act created no real right, either of ownership or security over the property. The Notice was also not an execution of any form of diligence and the fact that the only effect of registration of a notice was the creation of a new obligant meant that it could not be regarded as an instance of execution directed to the enforcement of the original obligation in terms of section12. Thus the Notice did not interrupt the operation of prescription nor render the obligation one relating to land.

As we shall see below, the court in this case ultimately held that the factoring charges in this particular case did not constitute a running account, and so each account was a separate obligation and prescribed independently of any other. Whether that conclusion is correct might be the matter of further debate, as the point does not appear to have been examined in detail.

Repayment of social security benefits were considered in *Cullen –v- Advocate General for Scotland*[49] where a social security recipient raised a petition seeking declarator that her obligation to repay £20,836.96 of income support had prescribed. The obligation had arisen as a result of the pursuer having claimed benefits to which she was not entitled over a period of time.

In March 2008 the Secretary of State had made a determination under the Social Security Administration Act 1992 that he was entitled to recover the sums. In 2016 the petitioner's wages were arrested pursuant to the 2008 determination. The petitioner denied any wrongdoing and had originally sought to appeal the determination, but failed due to the appeal having been lodged late.

It was argued for the pursuer that the obligation to repay benefits received by misrepresentation fell within Sch.1 para.1(b) of the 1973 Act as a form of unjustified enrichment and was therefore subject to prescription after the elapse of five years, which had commenced on the date of the Secretary of State's decision on 6 March 2008. If that were the case the claim would accordingly have prescribed on 6 March 2013.

The court concluded that in order to qualify as a claim for unjustified enrichment, the claim required to be grounded in equity. The claim made by the Secretary of State in his determination had a statutory origin and could not therefore fall within the definition of unjustified enrichment:-

> "*... the purpose and effect of section 71 and its predecessors was to create rights and obligations referable to the statutory powers conferred. In these circumstances, I conclude that, in contrast to redress for unjustified enrichment, which is a common law remedy grounded in equity (cf. Bell, Principles of the Law of Scotland, 10th edition,*

49 2017 SLT 1

> *paragraph 531) , the power conferred by section 71 , and the corresponding obligation to repay, are creations of public law."*[50]

As the social security legislation was designed to operate "outwith the scope of moral judgment" and thus could not be said to provide an equitable remedy, it could not be unjustified enrichment, which was a creature of equity. Section 6 of the 1973 Act accordingly did not apply and the Petition could not succeed.

As shall be seen below, the application of the 20-year prescriptive period to overpayments of UK-wide social security has been put beyond doubt in the Prescription (Scotland) Act 2018, albeit not without controversy.

Conclusion in Relation to the Prescriptive Periods

Schedule 3 of the 1973 Act contains an exhaustive list of those obligations which do not prescribe. Accordingly, where a right or obligation does not fit within one of the paragraphs of Schedule 3, it is subject to prescription in some way. The default position will be that the 20-year prescriptive period will apply unless the obligation falls within:

1. One of the subparagraphs of Schedule 1, paragraph 1 (as clarified by paragraph 2) (the five-year period);
2. Part II of the Act (limitation of actions);
3. Section 8A (the two-year period);
4. Section 22A (the ten-year period); or
5. Some other period specified in another enactment, such as planning or employment law legislation.

---

50 *per* Lord Armstrong, para 44

CHAPTER THREE
WHEN DOES THE CLOCK START TO RUN?

Introducing Sections 6 and 7 and Schedule 2

Having established which of the prescriptive periods apply to specific rights and obligations, the next question for the practitioner will usually be to identify the date from which the prescriptive period begins to run. This is not always straightforward.

Section 7 of the 1973 Act (which introduces the long negative prescription) states that the 20-year period will start "when any obligation to which this section applies has become enforceable". There does not appear to be any exception to that rule where the 20-year period applies.

By contrast, section 6 of the 1973 Act (which governs the short negative prescription) states that the prescriptive clock begins to run from the "appropriate date". Section 6(3) clarifies that the "appropriate date" means:-

> "*in relation to an obligation of any kind specified in Schedule 2 to this Act is a reference to the date specified in that Schedule in relation to obligations of that kind, and in relation to an obligation of any other kind is a reference to the date when the obligation became enforceable*"

Thus, in order to determine when the appropriate date is for an obligation subject to the short negative prescription, one must look firstly at Schedule 2 of the 1973 Act to determine whether the obligation falls within that schedule. If it does not, then the general rule applies and the prescriptive period will begin on the date upon which the obligation became enforceable. Generally, such questions will be a matter for proof.[1]

It will be remembered that Section 7 is said to apply to obligations including those under Section 6. The prescriptive period for obligations under Section 7 will always commence from the date that the obligation becomes enforceable. For obligations under Section 6, however, the period might also commence on the date specified in Schedule 2 (where applicable). That leads to a slight possibility that the two periods, each relating to the same obligation, might commence at different times. Whilst that will usually be of very little practical significance, it is to be borne in mind when the backstop function of Section 7 described above is being considered.

When relying upon "the date upon which the obligation became enforceable" it is important to be clear as to precisely what that date is. For example, in *Alton B Copeland Ltd –v- Orkney Builders (Contractors) Ltd*[2] a subcontractor sought payment of a balance due in respect of works carried out under contract to the defender, who was the main contractor on a building project. In terms of the contract, the pursuer submitted valuations which were in turn submitted to the ultimate client under the contract for approval. The defender had paid only part of the final valuation under the contract. It was argued by the defender that payment was due upon the submission of the valuation, which had occurred more than five years prior to the raising of the action. The Lord Ordinary (as he then was) disagreed with the defender's analysis. It was held that the defender had failed to establish that payment was due upon submission of the valuation:

> *"I reject the plea of prescription. ABC's final valuation was dated 12 December 2003; but it has not been demonstrated that the amount claimed in that valuation was enforceable as soon as ABC submitted the valuation to OB. ABC was the subcontractor of OB and it was*

1 See, e.g., *Deans -v- Thus plc,* 2005 SCLR 148

2 [2010] CSOH 135

its practice to submit an application for payment to OB for inclusion in OB's application to its employer. Thereafter, the employer's professional advisers would confirm what in their opinion was due to be paid and a certified sum would be paid to OB, which in turn would pay ABC. Counsel did not explore in evidence or in submission whether, under this contract, ABC had a right to sue OB for payment at any time before the subcontract works had been certified by the employer's advisers or before the employer had paid OB. I infer that it did not… But, in any event, OB has not demonstrated that the obligation to pay the sum claimed in ABC's final valuation of 12 December 2003 was enforceable before 12 January 2004. Accordingly the plea of prescription must fail"[3]

An interesting facet of this case is that the Lord Ordinary clearly considered the burden of proof to rest with the defenders. As we shall see below, the Prescription (Scotland) Act 2018 may have led to a different result.

Before considering the date upon which the obligation became enforceable, it is prudent to have regard to the terms of Schedule 2 of the 1973 Act. An examination of Schedule 2 now follows.

Schedule 2

Schedule 2 encompasses four types of obligation and sets out for each the date which is to be deemed the appropriate date for the purposes of Section 6.

A Series of Transactions

The first type of obligation under Schedule 2 is described as follows:-

3 Per Lord Hodge, at para [10]

> "*any obligation, not being part of a banking transaction, to pay money in respect of: (a) goods supplied on sale or hire, or (b) services rendered, in a series of transactions between the same parties (whether under a single contract or under several contracts) and charged on continuing account*"[4]

This definition is said to include goods supplied on Hire Purchase, credit sale or conditional sale. However, reference to "services rendered" is not to include "the work of keeping the account in question".[5] This last provision is designed to prevent a creditor from delaying the start of the prescriptive period by withholding the preparation of the account.

Where this provision applies, the appropriate date will be the date on which payment for the goods last supplied, or, as the case may be, the services last rendered, became due.[6] The due date for payment may not always be obvious. In *Johnston & Smart (Projects) Ltd –v- Sinclair*[7] for example services were provided by the pursuer over a 13-year period and on a continuing account basis. A "final account" was requested, and duly provided. An action was later raised and was served on the defender just over five years after the final account was rendered. The pursuer averred that the payment terms in relation to the final account were 30 days. Accordingly, it was argued, the pursuer could not sue on the account until 30 days had elapsed and so that was the date from which prescription should be calculated. This analysis was rejected by the court. The question was not when enforcement of payment could take place, but rather when the payment became "due". Payment was due upon the invoice being rendered and so it was held that the claim in this case had prescribed.

4 1973 Act, Schedule 2, para 1(1)

5 1973 Act, Schedule 2, para 1(2)

6 1973 Act, Schedule 2, para 1(4)

7 [2011] CSOH 166

There is some authority which suggests that in determining whether a series of transactions has taken place for these purposes, the court may have some regard to the manner in which the creditor keeps his records. Thus if their invoices make clear that the transaction is being charged on a running account, the court may take that into consideration.[8] This approach has been criticised, however.[9]

Likewise, a court is unlikely to hold that a matter is charged on a continuing account if it is clear that the creditor had treated the transactions as separate in the lead up to court proceedings. In *R Peter & Co Ltd -v- Pancake Place Ltd*[10] the pursuer was a builder seeking payment in respect of three invoices for works on three different premises. Two of those invoices had been rendered more than five years prior to the raising of proceedings. It was argued for the pursuer that those invoices formed part of a series of transactions rendered on a continuing account, and accordingly prescription had not run. The court identified that there had never been a consolidated demand for payment of the three invoices and nor were there any other facts which might suggest that the pursuer had deemed the transactions to be part of a continuing account. The earlier two invoices were accordingly held to have prescribed. That outcome can be contrasted with *HG Robertson -v- Murray International Metals Ltd*[11] where the court accepted at debate that averments of a series of transactions were sufficient to proceed to proof. The key to success appears to be competent drafting coupled with firm evidence of the intent of the parties.

Whilst payment of wages might be analysed as an obligation to make payment for services rendered. It has been held that this is not the case. *Reid –v- Beaton*[12] concerned a counterclaim for wages, some of which

8 See *GJ Van der Bent BV -v- Young & McMillan plc*, 2000 SLT (Sh Ct) 74

9 See for example D. Johnston, *Prescription & Limitation* (2nd Edition), W. Green, 2012, at para 6.66

10 1993 SLT 322

11 1998 SLT 747

12 1993 SCLR 382

fell due more than five years prior to the raising of the counterclaim. It was argued for the claimant that the wages were a continuing account for payment of services rendered and accordingly the prescriptive period ran from the last date upon which wages were payable. The Sheriff Principal disagreed. It was held that the obligation to pay wages was enforceable week by week. Each pay day was accordingly a separate and distinct claim. Those sums due for more than five years had accordingly prescribed.

There are other examples of supplies of services which might be considered to be provided on a "running account" basis, but which may not be. One example is property factoring charges. In *Cumbernauld Housing Partnership –v- Davies*[13] the defender appealed to the Inner House against the decision of the Sheriff Principal to grant Decree against her for payment of property factoring charges. Having held that the five-year negative prescription applied to the relevant charges, it is fair to say that the court did not enter into an in-depth examination of whether the charges were services rendered in a series of transactions, and it is not clear that this argument was laid before the court. The judgment therefore does not consider the question of whether Schedule 2, paragraph 1 might apply but instead appears to proceed on an assumption that each account stands on its own. Whether an argument based upon Schedule 2 might have succeeded will require to await a suitable future case, but this may be another example of where careful drafting might have availed a pursuer.

It is to be noted that the provision relates to payment for goods and services. It cannot be applied to a claim based on breach of contract in relation to those goods or services.[14]

The provision also specifically excludes banking transactions. "Banking transactions" are not defined within the Act, and nor does it appear to

---

13 2015 SC 532

14 *Beveridge & Kellas WS -v- Abercromby (no. 1)* 1997 SLT (Sh Ct) 5

be a recognised legal term. Most will fall within paragraph 2 (below), but there may be grey areas, such as vehicle or asset finance transactions which are both a form of lending, and also a hire purchase or conditional sale arrangement. At present there is little authority on the point.

Contracts of Loan or Deposit

The second type of obligation covered by Schedule 2 of the 1973 Act is:

> "*any obligation to repay the whole, or any part of, a sum of money lent to, or deposited with, the debtor under a contract of loan or, as the case may be, deposit.*"[15]

Where this provision applies, the Act stipulates two possible dates for the commencement of the prescriptive period.

First, where the contract contains a stipulation which provides for a date on or before which repayment of the sum (or part thereof) is to be made, the prescriptive period will run from the date on or before which that sum is to be repaid.[16]

Secondly, where the contract contains no such stipulation, but a written demand for repayment of the sum (or the part thereof), is made by or on behalf of the creditor to the debtor, the prescriptive period will commence on the date when such demand is made or first made.[17]

Those provisions are reasonably self-explanatory, although much will turn on the construction of the contract. It is to be noted that the provision relates not only to repayment of the full balance of a loan, but also to repayment of "any part of" that loan. A contract stipulating the precise dates upon which each instalment of a loan will fall due may

15 1973 Act, Schedule 2, paragraph 2(1)

16 1973 Act, Schedule 2, paragraph 2(2)(a)

17 1973 Act, Schedule 2, paragraph 2(2)(b)

theoretically have a number of different periods running in relation to each instalment.

The question of what constitutes a "written demand for repayment" is one which has been considered by the courts.

In *Bank of Scotland –v- Laverock*[18] the pursuer – a bank - sought payment of two debts due by the defender. More than five years prior to the action a judicial factor was appointed over the defender's estate, and the pursuer had lodged a claim with them. The defender argued that this claim amounted to a "written demand", and that the claim had accordingly expired. This argument was upheld at first instance. On appeal, it was held by the inner house that the claim did not constitute a demand and accordingly the prescriptive period did not start to run from the date of that claim.

In considering the use of the word "demand" within Schedule 2, the Court had recourse to the dictionary definition of "demand" and "claim", and pointed to the importance of there being no reference to repayment in the claim lodged with the judicial factor:

> "*As is plain from the dictionary definition already quoted, a demand involves a peremptory request or claim, and there is nothing peremptory in the language of the letter. The advertisement invited claims, and as the dictionary definition shows a claim is a demand for something as due or an assertion of a right to something. In my judgment the letter of 15th March 1979 was no more than an assertion by the pursuers of their rights in respect of these two bank accounts. It is significant that in the letter nothing whatsoever is expressly stated about repayment. Provided that payments of interest had been continued to be made in respect of the overdrafts, there is nothing in the letter to suggest that the pursuers wished the accounts to be closed by payment of the total sums outstanding. In my judgment there is a clear difference between a claim on the one hand*

---

18 1991 SC 117

> *and a demand for repayment in the other, and what one sees in the letter is simply a claim made in response to an invitation to intimate claims."* [19]

The provision applies to contracts of loan or deposit only. It has been held that this does not extend to personal guarantees or cautionary obligations relating to that loan.[20] For such obligations, prescription will run according to the general rule in Section 6 of the 1973 Act. In the case of a guarantee payable "on demand", that will be the date of the demand.[21]

Contracts of Partnership or Agency

The third type of obligation covered by Schedule 2 is described as:-

> *"any obligation under a contract of partnership or of agency, being an obligation remaining, or becoming, prestable on or after the termination of the relationship between the parties under the contract."*[22]

Where this provision applies, there are two possible dates. First, if the contract contains a stipulation with respect to the date on or before which performance of the obligation is to be due, prescription will begin to run from that date. Secondly, in any other case, prescription will run from the date that the relationship terminated.

Much will therefore turn on the interpretation of the contract of partnership or agency (if any). If the parties agree that an obligation be satisfied on a specific date or within a specific time after termination,

---

19 *Ibid. per* Lord-Justice Clerk (Ross), at p.125

20 *Royal Bank of Scotland Ltd -v- Brown* 1982 SC 89

21 *Ibid.*

22 1973 Act Schedule 2, para 3(1)

that will be the date that governs the prescriptive period. Otherwise it will run from the end of the relationship.

It is to be noted that the provision applies to obligations which remain or become prestable on or after termination. Obligations arising between partners during the currency of the partnership are not affected by this provision, although as we have already seen, such obligations are excluded from the short negative prescription by Schedule 1, paragraph 2. The 20-year period would accordingly apply to such obligations.

Payment by Instalments

Finally, Schedule 2 paragraph 4 provides a starting point for prescription in relation to:

> "*any obligation— (a) to pay an instalment of a sum of money payable by instalments, or (b) to execute any instalment of work due to be executed by instalments, not being an obligation to which any of the foregoing paragraphs applies.*"[23]

Where this provision applies, the appropriate date is "the date on which the last of the instalments is due to be paid or, as the case may be, to be executed."

The rule applies only to obligations to which none of the previous paragraphs of Schedule 2 apply. It would not, therefore, apply to contracts of loan or deposit. Nor would it apply to sale or hire agreements insofar as payable by instalments. It might potentially apply to building or construction contracts where works are ongoing and subject to staged payments.

Whilst it might sound obvious, the provision requires that an ascertainable sum of money be payable. In a case where there was loss due to a failure of an employer to enrol an employee in an insurance plan, but

23 1973 Act, Schedule 2, para 4(1)

the monetary value was unascertainable, the paragraph was held not to apply.[24]

Section 11

The commencement of the prescriptive period is not wholly governed by Sections 6 and 7 and schedule 2, however. In relation to reparation for loss, injury or damage, regard must also be had to Section 11.

Section 11 provides that:

> *"(1) Subject to subsections (2) and (3) below; any obligation (whether arising from any enactment, or from any rule of law or from, or by reason of any breach of, a contract or promise) to make reparation for loss, injury or damage caused by an act, neglect or default shall be regarded for the purposes of section 6 of this Act as having become enforceable on the date when the loss, injury or damage occurred.*
>
> *(2) Where as a result of a continuing act, neglect or default loss, injury or damage has occurred before the cessation of the act, neglect or default the loss, injury or damage shall be deemed for the purposes of subsection (1) above to have occurred on the date when the act, neglect or default ceased.*
>
> *(3) In relation to a case where on the date referred to in subsection (1) above (or, as the case may be, that subsection as modified by sub-section (2) above) the creditor was not aware, and could not with reasonable diligence have been aware, that loss, injury or damage caused as aforesaid had occurred, the said subsection (1) shall have effect as if for the reference therein to that date there were substituted a reference to the date when the creditor first became, or could with reasonable diligence have become, so aware."*

---

24 *Flynn -v- UNUM Ltd* 1996 SLT 1067

The general rule is that prescription starts to run from the coincidence of *damnum* (i.e. the wrongful act or omission) and *injuria* (being the loss and damage caused by the act or omission). Both elements must be present in order to found a claim. They date of the coincidence of *damnum* and *injuria* is not always obvious or easy to determine.[25] This date can potentially be extended by Section 11(3), however.

For the purposes of subsection 2, it is deemed that *damnum* and *injuria* will coincide upon the cessation of the continuing wrongful act. However, there is authority within the Sheriff Court to the effect that a claimant does not require to await the cessation of the ongoing act before raising proceedings.[26]

As we shall come to, Section 11(3) has had a significant amount of judicial attention recently, and has become one of the main drivers for reform. This is examined in some detail below, but for present purposes it is to be noted that knowledge of the loss injury or damage alone is sufficient for the prescriptive period to begin running.

Conclusions in Relation to the Start of the Prescriptive Period

For practitioners approaching a potential claim, it is clearly of some importance to be aware not only of the prescriptive period which applies, but also the date upon which that period commenced.

The starting point will depend upon the type of claim being pursued.

---

25 See, e.g., *Hunthaven Properties Limited -v- Hunter Construction (Aberdeen) Ltd,* [2017] CSOH 57 where the coincidence was said to have occurred upon a failure to make good certain defects and not upon the defects themselves. See also *Pelagic Freezing Ltd -v- Lovie Construction Ltd* [2010] CSOH 145.

26 *Weatherford Switzerland Trading & Development GmbH -v- iiiTEC Ltd*, [2019] SC ABE 87, although see also the dictum (obiter) of Lord Glennie in *Warren James (Jewellers) Ltd -v- Overgate GP Ltd* [2010] CSOH 57, at para [5], which appears to take a contrary view.

For claims of reparation for loss injury or damage, reference must be made to Section 11 of the 1973 Act. For all other claims it is suggested that the starting point ought to be Schedule 2, for the practitioner to determine whether the claim they intend to make is one which might fall within one of those paragraphs.

Where Schedule 2 does not apply, the key is to determine when the obligation in question became enforceable. That may not always be obvious and may require an examination of the underlying contract or invoices.

Finally, in cases where the long negative prescription applies to the obligation, Schedule 2 will never apply and regard may only be had to the date upon which the obligation became enforceable.

CHAPTER FOUR
INTERRUPTION AND SUSPENSION OF THE PRESCRIPTIVE PERIODS

Having established which prescriptive period applies and when it starts to run from, some thought must now be given to the question of whether the period has been interrupted in any way.

In terms of the Act there are two main ways in which a prescriptive period may be interrupted, resulting in a fresh period commencing. Those two ways are, broadly:

- A relevant claim having been made in relation to the obligation within the prescriptive period; and
- A relevant acknowledgment of the obligation having been given by the debtor within the prescriptive period.

In addition to those two ways of interrupting the period, Section 6(4) of the 1973 Act provides that:-

> "*In the computation of a prescriptive period in relation to any obligation for the purposes of this section—*
>
> *(a) any period during which by reason of—*
>
> *(i) fraud on the part of the debtor or any person acting on his behalf, or*
>
> *(ii) error induced by words or conduct of the debtor or any person acting on his behalf, the creditor was induced to refrain from making a relevant claim in relation to the obligation, and*

(b) any period during which the original creditor (while he is the creditor) was under legal disability,

shall not be reckoned as, or as part of, the prescriptive period:

Provided that any period such as is mentioned in paragraph (a) of this subsection shall not include any time occurring after the creditor could with reasonable diligence have discovered the fraud or error, as the case may be, referred to in that paragraph."

Accordingly, fraud, error or legal disability can also operate to prevent or suspend the running of the prescriptive period. It is to be noted that this is a suspension and not a new period – upon the suspension coming to an end, only the balance of any previously running prescriptive period will remain.

These elements are examined in more detail below.

Relevant Claims

Section 9 of the 1973 Act, provides a starting point in relation to relevant claims.

It provides that a 'relevant claim' means a claim made by or on behalf of the creditor for implement or part-implement of the obligation. The inclusion of the words "part implement" might be considered significant. Again, much could turn on the drafting of the writ or defences and one can envisage cases where argument is heard over whether a claim is part implement of a wider obligation, or implement of one in a series of individual obligations.

Section 9 then goes on to provide specification as to the forms of claim which constitute a "relevant claim". These are[1]:

1 See 1973 Act, Section 9(1) and its subparagraphs.

(a) A claim made in appropriate proceedings. "Appropriate proceedings" is further defined in Section 4 of the 1973 Act and means one of three things: (i) proceedings in a court of competent jurisdiction in Scotland or elsewhere, other than a Court of Session action initiated by a Summons which is not subsequently called; (ii) any arbitration in Scotland in respect of which an arbitrator (or panel of arbitrators) has been appointed; or (iii) any arbitration in a country other than Scotland where an arbitration award would be enforceable in Scotland.

It is to be noted that in the case of an arbitration, the claim will be deemed to have been made when the arbitration begins.[2] That is either when the parties agree that it begins[3], or when a party to an arbitration agreement gives the other party notice submitting the dispute to arbitration.[4]

However, an agreement or formal notice of referral of a matter to arbitration which does not actually proceed to an arbitration is not sufficient to constitute a relevant claim.[5] That leads to a potential anomaly: a notice of referral to arbitration begins the process and will interrupt prescription where the matter then proceeds to arbitration. However, in the intervening period between the notice and the appointment of arbitrators the question of prescription appears to be in limbo. There does not appear to be any judicial authority as to the status of the claim during that period. Nor do the Scottish Arbitration Rules provide for a long stop date by which an arbitrator must be appointed (albeit either party can require the other to agree an

2 1973 Act, Section 9(3)

3 1973 Act, Section 4(4)(a)

4 Arbitration (Scotland) Act 2010, Schedule 1 (Scottish Arbitration Rules), Rule 1.

5 John O'Connor (Plant Hire) Limited –v- Kier Construction Ltd, 1990 SCLR 761

appointee within 28 days by giving notice).[6] Theoretically, the prescriptive period might be in limbo for some time.

In a case where a party sought to rely upon a reference to the Financial Ombudsman Service (FOS) as being a referral of a matter to a form of arbitration, if was held that an ombudsman was not equivalent to an arbitrator and a plea to prescription was upheld.[7] A key consideration was the binding nature of the arbitration process on the parties. A decision of the FOS was not binding on the complainer, who could choose to reject it and pursue their claim in other ways.[8]

For actions in the Scottish Courts proceedings are commenced upon citation of the defender.[9] In relation to Court of Session actions, however, citation will only interrupt prescription if the summons subsequently calls.[10] The summons will fall after a year and a day from the date of expiry of the period of notice if not lodged for calling.[11] If the claim would prescribe between the citation of the defender and the calling of the summons, then (as with arbitration) that period appears to be a form of legal Schrödinger's cat, where a claim can be both prescribed and not prescribed. Whether the claim has indeed prescribed is dependent upon whether a future action (the calling of the summons) occurs. There is, of course, provision for an

---

6 Arbitration (Scotland) Act 2010, Schedule 1 (Scottish Arbitration Rules), Rule 6

7 *Clark -v- Argyle Consulting Ltd,* 2011 SLT 180

8 Whilst outside the scope of this book, there is English authority to the effect that where a FOS decision is accepted by the parties, it may found a plea of *res judicata*: *Clark & Another -v- In Focus Asset Management* [2014] EWCA 118. This suggests FOS decisions might be considered "judicial" in certain circumstances, in particular where the outcome is accepted by the complainer.

9 See, e.g., The Hon Lord Macphail, *Sheriff Court Practice* (3rd Edition, W. Green, 2006), at para 6.06

10 See *Barclay -v- Chief Constable of the Northern Constabulary*, 1986 SLT 562

11 Rules of the Court of Session, rule 13.13(6)

opponent to force the issue within the year and a day,[12] but a certain amount of legal limbo may still arise.

(b) Presentation of or concurrence in a petition for the sequestration of a debtor, or the submission of a claim in a sequestration under Section 46 or 122 of the Bankruptcy (Scotland) Act 2016.

(c) A claim made by a creditor to a trustee acting under a protected trust deed for creditors.

(d) Presentation of or concurrence in a petition for the winding up of a company, or by the submission of a claim in a liquidation in terms of Section 411 of the Insolvency Act 1986.

(e) The execution by or on behalf of a creditor in an obligation of any form of diligence directed to the enforcement of the obligation. "Diligence" can be a difficult concept to define.[13] It has been held that an inhibition constitutes diligence, and interrupts prescription from the date of registration.[14] However, registration of a Notice of Potential Liability under the Tenements (Scotland) Act 2004 does not constitute diligence.[15] In the Outer House of the Court of Session it has been held that service of an arrestment to found jurisdiction was not sufficient to commence an action, and that service of the summons would

---

12 Rules of the Court of Session, rule 13.14

13 See, for example, the discussion in *Lord Advocate -v- Royal Bank of Scotland Ltd*, 1977 SC 155 (although caution should be exercised given subsequent reforms to the law of diligence).

14 *Hogg -v- Prentice*, 1994 SCLR 426 – N.B. this case involved inhibition on the dependence, but it is submitted the principle also applies to inhibition in execution.

15 *Cumbernauld Housing Partnership Limited -v- Davies*, 2015 SC 532

be required. The view was expressed that an arrestment on the dependence would likewise be of no effect.[16]

In the case of rights relating to property which are subject to the long negative prescription under Section 8, the expression "relevant claim" not only means a claim made by or on behalf of the creditor to establish a right, but can also mean proceedings to contest any claim to a right inconsistent therewith.[17] This might apply, for example, where an action is raised for declarator of a servitude right, and a defence is lodged.

Where proceedings are raised, it seems that a non-material defect in the claimant's designation will not invalidate the claim, such as where a pursuer is acting in his capacity as trustee, but fails to design himself as such.[18] Likewise, where a party's whole business and undertaking is transferred to another party during the course of proceedings, the new party may be brought into the action without prescription being engaged.[19]

Where court proceedings are raised and subsequently dismissed, this may competently interrupt the prescriptive period. This appears to be the case even if the earlier proceedings are lacking in relevancy.[20] Where the merits of a claim have been considered and ruled upon at proof, however, the rule does not prevent a plea of *res judicata* in any subsequent action and will not operate where decree of absolvitor in a previous action has been pronounced.[21]

---

16 *RM Supplies (Inverkeithing) Limited –v- EMS Trans Schiffahrisges GmbH*, 2003 SLT 133

17 1973 Act, Section 9(2)

18 *Royal Insurance UK Ltd –v- Amec Construction Scotland Ltd*, 2008 SLT 825

19 *Friends Provident Life Assurance Ltd -v- Robert McAlpine Ltd,* [2014] CSOH 74

20 *Thomas Menzies (Builders) Ltd -v- Anderson & Menzies* 1988 SLT 794

21 See, e.g., *Mazur -v- Mitchells Roberton* 2018 GWD 37-459

Amending in a new claim to an existing action within the prescriptive period will itself constitute a relevant claim, even if the amendment is not formally allowed until after the prescriptive period has expired.[22] Indeed the period may be interrupted merely by intimation of the Minute, even if not lodged with the court until after the expiry of the period.[23] In a case where a party's plea in law was framed in such a way as to be clear that a remedy was being sought, it was held that this gave sufficient notice to the party's opponent and might constitute a relevant claim notwithstanding the fact that there was no formal conclusion or crave for the remedy before the court.[24] It is not enough, however, to intimate a legal aid application setting out an intention to amend upon the granting of legal aid for that purpose.[25]

There is some doubt as to the extent to which raising a declaratory action will constitute a "relevant claim". In *Wylie –v- Avon Insurance*[26] it was held that an action seeking declarator in relation to the terms of a policy of insurance was not sufficient to interrupt prescription in order to allow indemnification for a specific incident. This can be contrasted with *Highland & Islands Airports Ltd –v- Shetland Islands Council*[27] where it was argued that the Summons, which sought only declaratory conclusions and contained no conclusion for specific implement nor payment of money was sufficient to interrupt prescription.

The crucial element appears to be careful framing of the declarator sought, as well as the averments and pleas in order to leave no room for doubt that a relevant claim is being made. In *Highland & Islands Airports*, the court considered that averments of loss and damage which

---

22 *Kinnaird –v- Donaldson*, 1992 SCLR 694;

23 *Gillies -v- Arjo Wiggin Limited and another*, [2019] SAC(Civ) 034; see also *Link Housing Association Ltd -v- PBL Construction Ltd*, 2009 SC 653

24 *Ecclesiastical Insurance Office plc -v- Whitehouse-Grant-Christ*, 2016 SLT 990

25 *Yeboah –v- Glasgow Caledonian University*, 2016 G.W.D. 25-455

26 1988 SCLR 570

27 2015 SC 588

went on to explain that the full extent of the loss and damage could not then be quantified due to the complexity of the claim was sufficient to point to a relevant claim being made. As the then Lord President put it:

> *"In a case such as this the question whether a declaratory conclusion constitutes the making of a relevant claim falls to be determined by reference to the terms in which declarator is sought and to the condescendence and pleas in law that support it. That, I think, reflects the view that there should be a practical rather than a technical approach to the interpretation of the 1973 Act … In this case, the declarators sought directly impute contractual and delictual liabilities to the defender. The condescendence then specifies in detail the contract on which the action is founded, the duties on the part of the defender to which the contract gave rise, and the respects in which the defender is said to have been in breach of the contract and of certain duties of care. It then expressly avers that these breaches have caused the pursuer to sustain financial loss for which the pursuer seeks damages; and that by reason of the complexity of the claim, the damages cannot yet be precisely quantified. The basis of the claim is then epitomised in the pleas in law."*[28]

What is clear throughout this area of law is that success or failure where a plea to prescription is taken can often depend on the skill of the person preparing the written pleadings, and a prudent practitioner must give careful consideration to his or her claim before putting pen to paper.

Regardless of the form which it takes, where a court action is raised within the prescriptive period but is then not pursued for an inordinate and excessive period of time, the court has an inherent power to bring it to an end and to grant decree of absolvitor in relation to the claim.[29]

---

28 *Ibid, per Lord President (Gill)* at p 592

29 *Tonner -v- Reiach & Hall,* 2008 SC 1

Relevant Acknowledgements

The concept of a "relevant acknowledgment" is defined in Section 10(1) of the 1973 Act which states that:

> *"The subsistence of an obligation shall be regarded for the purposes … this Act as having been relevantly acknowledged if, and only if, either of the following conditions is satisfied, namely—*
>
> *(a) that there has been such performance by or on behalf of the debtor towards implement of the obligation as clearly indicates that the obligation still subsists;*
>
> *(b) that there has been made by or on behalf of the debtor to the creditor or his agent an unequivocal written admission clearly acknowledging that the obligation still subsists."*

The question might arise as to the position where two or more people are liable jointly and severally, but the relevant acknowledgement is only made by one of them. Section 10(2) of the 1973 Act provides the answer to that. It states that where the acknowledgement has been by way of performance of or towards the obligation, this will be binding on all co-obligants. If the acknowledgement has been made by way of written admission, this will only bind the person making the admission. This of course has the unhappy side effect whereby two different prescriptive periods may start to run for the same obligation.

In the case of a debt, "performance by or on behalf of the debtor" usually means making a payment towards the debt. Where the debt or other obligation has been assigned to a new creditor, performance by the debtor in favour of the new creditor not only interrupts prescription, but also appears to negate the need for intimation of the assignation.[30]

---

30 *Inverlochy Castle Ltd –v- Lochaber Power Co.*, 1987 SLT 466

It has been argued that payment of a sum of money on its own cannot be taken as an acknowledgement of anything beyond that sum of money being due. That position has not upheld by the courts, however.[31] The principle appears to be that subsistence of the obligation is severable from the question of quantum of a claim. Performance towards an obligation does not necessarily denote agreement on the value of the obligation, nor even on liability, but merely interrupts prescription. Parties are therefore still free to argue over liability and quantum.

In cases where a party relies upon a written acknowledgement rather than due performance of the debt, any written acknowledgement must be clear and unequivocal. The test is a high one.

In a case where a letter was issued after the date for performance of an obligation had passed, which intimated that performance of the obligation would not be possible, this was not held to be an unequivocal admission that the obligation existed, but rather an intimation that performance was impossible, which the court considered to be a different proposition.[32]

It does not avoid the provision, however, that a party marks an unequivocal admission of an obligation as being "without prejudice". Such an unequivocal admission can be considered and taken account of by the court.[33]

Likewise, the making of payments to a party "without admission of liability" or under reservation of rights will not necessarily prevent the court from holding that a relevant acknowledgement has taken place.[34] In *Wilkie* a party claimed under a policy of insurance for a fire at his

31 *Wilkie –v- Direct Line Insurance (no.2),* 2002 SLT 530, also briefly discussed in *Cumbernauld Housing Partnership –v- Davies*, 2015 SC 532

32 *Liebermann –v- GW Tait & Sons SSC*, 1987 SC 213

33 *Richardson –v- Quercus Ltd*, 1999 SC 278

34 *Wilkie –v- Direct Line Insurance (No. 2),* 2002 SLT 530

premises. The insurer, whilst making investigations, paid for him to be put in alternative accommodation and made certain other interim payments, all of which were said to be made on an *ex gratia* basis and without admission as to liability under the policy. Sometime later, the insurer repudiated the policy and declared it void due to certain misrepresentations said to have been made at the inception of the policy. The question was whether the payments made by the insurer – made *ex gratia* and without admission of liability – were sufficient to interrupt prescription. The court held that they did:

> "*the contention on behalf of the pursuer was that the payments which were made, in particular the payment for his accommodation until 28 May, indicated to him, and judged objectively would have indicated to anyone in his position, that the defenders accepted a present liability under the policy even if they reserved the right to withdraw such acceptance at some stage in the future. I have come to the view that that contention is sound.*"[35]

The test accordingly appears to be an objective one: what indications as to the debtor's position should one should take from the fact that interim payments are being made, notwithstanding the reservation of rights.

Fraud, Error or Legal Disability

As set out above, where a party pleads that they were induced to refrain from making a relevant claim due to fraud error or legal disability, it will operate to suspend the prescriptive period for so long as the error or disability continues. It does not interrupt the prescriptive period and begin a new one.

The concept is set out in Section 6(4) of the 1973 Act, which provides as follows:

---

35 *Ibid, per* Lord Kingarth, at p. 536

> *"In the computation of a prescriptive period in relation to any obligation for the purposes of this section—*
>
> *(a) any period during which by reason of—*
>
> *(i) fraud on the part of the debtor or any person acting on his behalf, or*
>
> *(ii) error induced by words or conduct of the debtor or any person acting on his behalf,*
>
> *the creditor was induced to refrain from making a relevant claim in relation to the obligation, and*
>
> *(b) any period during which the original creditor (while he is the creditor) was under legal disability,*
>
> *shall not be reckoned as, or as part of, the prescriptive period: Provided that any period such as is mentioned in paragraph (a) of this subsection shall not include any time occurring after the creditor could with reasonable diligence have discovered the fraud or error, as the case may be, referred to in that paragraph."*

The provision applies only to the short negative prescription, and there is no equivalent provision in Section 7 in relation to long negative prescription. Where the long negative prescription has started to run (bearing in mind, as discussed above that the 20-year period also applies as a long-stop to claim under the short negative prescription), the claim will prescribe after 20 years regardless of the existence of fraud, error or legal disability. That issue does not appear to have been tested, but would appear to be the import of the interrelation between sections 6 and 7 and the precise meaning of "*computation of a prescriptive period in relation to any obligation <u>for the purposes of this section</u>*" in Section 6(4).

That point aside, the provision is reasonably self-explanatory, although there are a number of principles which can be gleaned from case law.

In the first place, it is clear that whether or not a conscious choice by a party is made not to press their claim is unimportant. Rather what is required is that a claim is competent, but not pursued by reason of the fraud or error. Put another way:

> *"I would hold therefore that the period of time covered by the word 'refrain' in sec 6(4) includes time when the creditor does nothing to enforce the obligation, whether or not this is the result of a conscious decision on his part not to press the claim. As my noble and learned friend Lord Millett has said, it is not necessary for the creditor to identify the date when he would have made the claim but for the error. But the prescriptive period will only be interrupted if he can show that the reason why he did nothing to enforce the claim against the debtor was because he was misled by the debtor's fraud or by error induced by the debtor's words or conduct. And, under the proviso to sec 6(4) , the period of the interruption will not include any time after he could with reasonable diligence have discovered the fraud or error."*[36]

It also appears that the words or conduct inducing the error cannot be the same words or conduct which founds the claim itself.[37] Moreover, where a misrepresentation is claimed resulting in error and a failure to raise proceedings, that will usually be seen as a single act rather than a continuing wrong which is ongoing until the misrepresentation is corrected. To do otherwise would extend the prescriptive period until the misrepresentation was corrected by the debtor. Such a situation has been described by one sheriff as "an illicit attempt to circumvent the 1973 Act".[38]

If the person inducing the error or perpetrating the fraud is in a fiduciary relationship with the party who might otherwise have a claim, the

36 *BP Exploration Operating Company Ltd –v- Chevron Transport*, 2002 SC(HL) 19, per Lord Hope of Craighead at p.30

37 *Macdonald -v- Clydesdale Bank plc*, [2017] SC EDIN 65

38 *Ibid*, at para [32]

court may take account of the conflict of interest in determining whether Section 6(4) applies. In *Dryburgh –v- Scotts Media Tax Limited*[39] a director was in breach of his fiduciary duty by carrying out certain transactions and paying dividends to himself. At first instance it was found that a claim by the company had prescribed. On appeal, it was held by the Inner House that prescription did not run between the period when the wrongful acts took place and the winding up of the company four years later.

> *"[W]e should make two general observations. First, the exception to the general rule of prescription that is found in that subsection must in our opinion be construed purposively, in such a way as to give effect to the clear objectives of the subsection. Those can be ascertained by reference to the circumstances to which the language of the statute relates and external factors such as the policy that underlies it. Secondly, throughout the period between the September transactions and the winding up of SMT the respondent was a director of the company and consequently stood in a fiduciary position towards it. This is important. A fundamental principle applies to all fiduciary relationships: a fiduciary may not place himself in a position where his interest and his duty may possibly conflict, and if he does so he is obliged to account for any loss to his principal, or to make good any loss suffered by his principal"*[40]

More recently it has been held that "conduct" may be construed in a wide sense, and may include passivity as well as positive conduct by a party inducing error. *Heather Capital Limited (in liquidation) –v- Levy & Macrae*[41] was an action alleging breach of trust and negligence against two firms of solicitors by the liquidator of a company. The facts involved allegations of fraud on behalf of officers of the company and "dishonest assistance" on the part of the solicitors. It was argued (partially successfully) by the defenders at first instance that certain claims

39 2014 SC 651

40 *Ibid, Per* Lord Drummond Young at p.657

41 2017 SLT 376

had prescribed. The pursuer appealed to the Inner House. In the course of their judgment (which allowed the appeal) the Court considered section 6(4), and in particular the word "conduct". The judgment provides a helpful summary of where the law currently stands:

> "'*Conduct' is not defined in the 1973 Act. The approach to s.6(4) adopted by the courts suggests that the word should not be construed in a narrow or restrictive way.... Adopting that approach, it is my opinion that relevant conduct in the context of prescription may be active or passive. It may involve positive action, but equally, in certain circumstances, it may involve a silence or a lack of action. The conduct need not be deliberate, or blameworthy, or careless, or be carried out with any particular motive such as deception or concealment... The conduct does not have to constitute a crime or a breach of duty (whether contractual or delictual or fiduciary)... The conduct does not require to be the sole cause of the error... It follows from the above that the relevant question, in my opinion, is simply whether any conduct on the part of the solicitors concerned, viewed objectively, induced or contributed to inducing some or all of the error as defined above, with the result that HC refrained (in the broad sense explained in BP Exploration) from making any claim against the solicitors.*"[42]

This is, of course, potentially very wide. In particular, it suggests that silence can be construed as "conduct" and can therefore suspend the running of prescription. It makes clear that the motives of the debtor are unimportant, and that the conduct need not be the sole cause of error. Taken to its logical conclusion, if one is inadvertently silent on a matter where the creditor decides not to pursue for a variety of reasons (the silence being one of those reasons), that may be sufficient to prevent prescription running.

---

42 *Ibid, per* Lady Paton at p. 390

CHAPTER FIVE
REPARATION FOR LOSS, INJURY OR DAMAGE – THE DISCOVERABILITY TEST

One of the major issues to arise in the recent judicial treatment of this area of law, and one of the main catalysts to reform, is the so-called "discoverability test".

The discoverability test is found in Section 11 of the 1973 Act. This has been set out above, but bears repeating with some added emphasis:

> *"(1) Subject to subsections (2) and (3) below; any obligation (whether arising from any enactment, or from any rule of law or from, or by reason of any breach of, a contract or promise) to make reparation for loss, injury or damage caused by an act, neglect or default shall be regarded for the purposes of section 6 of this Act as having become enforceable on the date when the loss, injury or damage occurred.*
>
> *(2) Where as a result of a continuing act, neglect or default loss, injury or damage has occurred before the cessation of the act, neglect or default the loss, injury or damage shall be deemed for the purposes of subsection (1) above to have occurred on the date when the act, neglect or default ceased.*
>
> *(3) In relation to a case where on the date referred to in subsection (1) above (or, as the case may be, that subsection as modified by sub-section (2) above)* ***the creditor was not aware, and could not with reasonable diligence have been aware****, that loss, injury or damage* <u>***caused as aforesaid***</u> ***had occurred****, the said subsection (1) shall have effect as if for the reference therein to that date there were substituted*

> *a reference to the date when the creditor* ***first became, or could with reasonable diligence have become, so aware.***" (emphasis added)

In order to fully understand the significance of this provision, it is necessary first to take a historical view of the provision and how it was understood for many years before turning to examine some of the recent case law on the point.

Historical View of Discoverability Test

For many years the accepted approach to Section 11(3) was encapsulated in *Greater Glasgow Health Board –v- Baxter, Clark & Paul.*[1]

In this case a health board raised an action of damages against a firm of architects for alleged negligence by them in connection with the reconstruction of a hospital. The health board had appointed the architects in 1966. The reconstruction works had been executed between 1969 and 1971 by a building company with whom the health board had entered into a separate contract. Defects arose thereafter and the health board raised an action against the architects in 1982 although the health board had known that certain windows and certain areas of mosaic were defective in certain respects in 1972.

In 1978 parties had entered into a deed wherein the architects stated that: "As yet it has not been practicable to ascertain the full extent and nature of those defects and faults or the causes thereof or the amount of loss and damage suffered by the Board...or to have determined...whether such defects...had been caused wholly or in part through our fault and negligence...Therefore we agree that these presents shall constitute a 'relevant acknowledgment', within the meaning of" section 10 of the 1973 Act.

It was argued that the action had prescribed. The "acknowledgement" was not an acknowledgement as required under the 1973 Act as it did

1 1990 SC 237

not make clear that there was a subsisting obligation. In particular, it stated that the cause of the defects and the defender's liability for them was unknown.

The health board argued that the claim had not prescribed as they had not been aware and could not with reasonable diligence have become aware that they had sustained loss, injury or damage caused by the architects' negligence until after the date of the execution of the deed, in 1978, hence s.11(3) applied.

The court held that the obligation had indeed prescribed. In giving judgment, the court set out the law as it would stand for some considerable time thereafter.

> "*I have reached the view ... that sec. 11(3) requires knowledge that the loss, injury or damage was caused by negligence... I am not persuaded that sec. 11(3) is still available with a view to deferring the start of the prescriptive period when the creditor knows of the loss, knows that it was caused by negligence, but does not know the identity of the person on whom the obligation lies.*"[2]

In terms of this judgment, therefore it became understood that in order for prescription to start running in a claim for reparation what was required was:

- Knowledge that loss, injury or damage had been incurred; and
- Knowledge that this had been caused by negligence.

It was not required that the identity of the party who was responsible for the loss, injury or damage be known to the claimant.

Wilful ignorance on these points would not avail a claimant of any protection given that Subs (3) provides that it is not just actual awareness

2 *Ibid, per* Lord Clyde, at p.252

but the date where the creditor could "with reasonable diligence have become aware" which is of importance.

Lord Clyde's approach in *Baxter, Clark & Paul* was later approved by the Inner House in *Glasper –v- Rodger.*[3] That was a case in which solicitors were pursued by their former clients in relation to alleged negligence in that it was claimed that the solicitors had taken title to a hotel premises in their son's name and not their own, a fact which they were unaware of until some time later. The Lord President approved the approach of Lord Clyde:

> "*In our opinion the lack of awareness which requires to be established for the purposes of section 11(3) of the 1973 Act is a lack of awareness that a loss has occurred caused by an act, neglect or default which gives rise to an obligation to make reparation for it. We agree with Lord Clyde's observation in* Greater Glasgow Health Board v Baxter Clark & Paul ... *that the subsection looks for an awareness not only of the fact of loss having occurred, but of the fact that it is a loss caused by negligence*"[4]

According to this principle then, the test of whether Section 11(3) applies to extend the start of the prescriptive period was:

- Does the claimant have knowledge of the loss, injury or damage?
- If they don't *actually* know about the loss, injury or damage, could they with reasonable diligence have become aware? and
- Is the claimant aware that the loss injury or damage was caused by fault or negligence, regardless of whether they know the identity of the negligent party?

---

3 1996 SLT 44

4 *Ibid, per* Lord President (Hope) at p. 47

If the answer to these questions is "no", the prescriptive period would be held not to have started to run.

Morrison -V- ICL Plastic and Beyond

Such was the state of the law when the Inner House heard the appeal in the case of *Morrison –v- ICL Plastics Ltd.*[5]

In that case the pursuers had raised proceedings for reparation following the destruction of their premises by an explosion at a neighbouring factory. The proceedings were raised more than five years following the explosion. It was argued for the pursuer that, whilst it was clear that loss and damage had occurred immediately, it was not immediately apparent that the loss had been caused by fault or negligence. That could only be determined following the conclusion of an inquiry into the explosion, which took several years.

At first instance the Lord Ordinary had held that the claim had indeed prescribed. In doing so the Lord Ordinary did not interfere with the reasoning in *Baxter* nor in *Glasper*, but rather held that in circumstances where damage was caused by an explosion the principle of *res ipsa loquitor* applied (i.e. the facts speak for themselves). It was considered to have been obvious to the creditor that some negligence might have been involved as factories do not routinely explode. On that basis, the Lord Ordinary held, the prescriptive period started to run immediately upon the explosion having occurred.

The Inner House allowed the pursuer's appeal and held that the claim had not prescribed. In doing so the Division underlined the applicability of the earlier case law and the principles derived from it:

> *"In the present case, one of the defenders' contentions is that the pursuers, on 11 May 2004, were not only immediately aware of their*

5 2013 SC 391

> *loss and damage as a result of the explosion but were also immediately aware (or could work on the assumption) that the explosion was caused by negligence. We do not agree. While an explosion in a building is a rare occurrence, and while, as the Lord Ordinary correctly observes at para 37 of his opinion, it provides a good basis for a writ averring* res ipsa loquitur... *the fact that there has been an explosion in a building does not, in our view, inevitably mean that it must have been caused by negligence. It is unnecessary for present purposes to list examples of non-negligent causes of explosions. However two were discussed during the debate. First, there may have been a deliberate act by a third party over whom the owners and occupiers had no control. Secondly, a previously unknown design fault in an underground pipe may have caused the explosion. In our view it is necessary in the present debate to keep the possibility of non-negligent causes in mind, and the fact that it may not be possible confidently to exclude non-negligent causes in every case without some investigation"*[6]

The defender appealed the matter to the UK Supreme Court.[7] The Supreme Court were split in their decision. The majority held that the claim had indeed prescribed, and in doing so overturned almost a quarter of a century of practice.

In the lead judgment the Supreme Court focussed on the use of the words "caused as aforesaid" where they occurred in Section 11(3). The question was whether the words "caused as aforesaid" meant that the claimant had to be aware only of the occurrence of the damage, or whether he had also to be aware that the damage had been caused by an act, neglect or default.

Lord Reed set out the position as follows:

---

6 *Ibid, per* Lady Paton at p.400

7 2014 SC (UKSC) 222

> *"[16] Section 11(3) of the 1973 Act is capable of being read in two different ways. One possibility is to read the word 'aware' as referring to the loss, injury or damage, and to treat the phrase 'caused as aforesaid' as adjectival. The subsection is then read as if it said: 'the creditor was not aware ... that loss, injury or damage,* ***which had been*** *caused as aforesaid, had occurred' (emphasis added). The creditor has then to be aware only of the occurrence of loss, while the words 'caused as aforesaid' connect the loss to the cause of action.*
>
> *[17] The other possibility is to read the word 'aware' as referring not only to the loss, injury or damage but also to the fact that it has been 'caused as aforesaid'. The subsection is then read as if it said: 'the creditor was not aware ... that loss, injury or damage had occurred, and that it had been caused as aforesaid' (emphasis added). Since the words 'caused as aforesaid' refer back to sec 11(1) and mean 'caused by an act, neglect or default', the creditor then has to be aware of a composite of fact and law, comprising the occurrence of loss and the act, neglect or default which caused it, actionability being an element of the concept of an act, neglect or default."*[8]

Having expressed the view that the first of these two interpretations seems the most in accordance with the ordinary English language, Lord Reed then went on to examine other sections of the 1973 Act to determine whether guidance may be sought from within the four corners of the statute:

> *"Although there are significant differences between prescription and limitation, the point can nevertheless be made that secs 18(3) and 22(2) illustrate that where it was intended that the limitation period was not to run so long as there was a lack of awareness of particular matters, the draftsman made it clear, by express language, what those matters were. If it had been Parliament's intention, in relation to sec 11(3) , that the prescriptive period was not to run so long as there was a lack of awareness of matters other than the occurrence of loss,*

8 *Ibid,* at p.228

injury and damage, one could reasonably expect that that would have been made equally clear."[9]

In light of these comments and his analysis, Lord Reed's conclusion is that all that is required under Section 11(3) to start the prescriptive clock is knowledge of loss and damage having been incurred – knowledge that it was caused by negligence is irrelevant The judgment is worth quoting in full:

> "*The interpretation of sec 11(3) which I prefer is… consistent with my initial impression that the subsection is intended to deal with latent damage. So understood, sec 11(3) follows the same approach as sec 11(1) and (2). The general rule laid down by sec 11(1) focuses on the occurrence of loss: the timing of its occurrence determines the date on which the prescriptive period begins. Section 11(2) addresses the problem which could otherwise arise where loss results from a continuing default, by providing a deemed date for the occurrence of loss, which is to be used instead of the actual date for the purposes of sec 11(1). Section 11(3) addresses the problem which could otherwise arise where there is latent damage, namely that the creditor is unaware of its occurrence, by requiring the date of actual or constructive knowledge of its occurrence to be used instead for the purposes of sec 11(1). If sec 11(3) is so interpreted, all three subsections share a common focus upon the occurrence and timing of loss.*
>
> *[26] There are two further, and in my opinion compelling, reasons for rejecting the interpretation of sec 11(3) favoured by Lord Clyde. The first is the sheer oddity of postponing prescription according to the creditor's knowledge that an act or omission is actionable. If he has to be aware that the loss was caused by an act, neglect or default, then it follows … that he has to be aware that there has been a breach of a legal duty owed to him, as was accepted in Greater Glasgow Health Board v Baxter, Clark and Paul and the other authorities I have mentioned. As it was put in Glasper v Rodger (p 47), the lack of*

9 *Ibid,* at p.229

awareness which requires to be established for the purposes of sec 11(3) is a lack of awareness that a loss has occurred caused by an act, neglect or default 'which gives rise to an obligation to make reparation for it.' That however results in a number of unlikely consequences.

[27] It means, in the first place, that prescription will run more or less quickly according to the creditor's awareness of the law. If he receives accurate advice from his solicitor, it will begin on one date; if the advice is inaccurate, it will begin on another. If there are a number of creditors who suffer loss as a result of the same event, their claims may prescribe on different dates, depending on the legal advice which they receive. That runs contrary to the legal certainty which is the objective of prescription, and seems unlikely to have been the intention of Parliament.

[28] More fundamentally, in what sense can the creditor be 'aware' that there has been a breach of duty, in advance of a judicial determination of the issue? Does being 'aware' require certainty of success in a claim, or probability, or something less? In practice, even if the creditor has received legal advice, he is likely, at best, to be aware only that he has good prospects of success. If the advice has been less optimistic, he may be aware that he has reasonable prospects of success, or that he has an arguable case."[10]

The majority of the Court agreed with Lord Reed (Lords Hodge and Toulson dissented), and accordingly the long-standing interpretation of Section 11(3) was overturned.

The position in relation to claims for reparation now is that the prescriptive period will start at the point when the creditor knows (or with reasonable diligence could have become aware) that they have suffered loss, injury and damage. There is no longer any requirement that they know or suspect that the loss has been caused by negligence, nor that

10 *Ibid,* at p.230

they are aware of the person against whom they might have a claim. Knowledge of the loss is all that is required.

This approach has since been upheld by the Court in further cases, most notably in *Gordon's Trustees –v- Campbell Riddell Breeze Paterson.*[11]

The *Gordon's Trustees* case involved an attempted termination of an agricultural tenancy. It appears that the relevant notices to quit were served negligently in 2004 and were ineffective due to certain inaccuracies in the notices. The tenants refused to vacate the fields upon expiry of the notices in 2005. The pursuer subsequently applied to the Land Court to seek the tenant's removal. The Land Court application was refused in 2008. An action for damages was raised four years after the final interlocutor in the Land Court application (in 2012), which was around eight years after the service of the notices and seven years after the notices ought to have expired.

It was accepted that only knowledge of loss was required in order for Section 11(3) to operate. However, it was argued that the Pursuer could not have been aware that they had suffered loss until the Land Court had finally refused the application, as until that point it was possible that the situation might be salvaged.

On this occasion the court were unanimous in their position, with Lord Hodge (having previously dissented in *Morrison*) giving the lead judgment. The main issue before the court was summarised by him as follows:-

> "*In* Morrison v ICL *this court did not have to address the question which this appeal raises, namely whether in section 11(3) the creditor must be able to recognise that he has suffered some form of detriment before the prescriptive period begins. In* Morrison v ICL *the property damage was manifest on the date of the explosion. But where a client*

---

11 2017 SLT 1287

> *of a professional adviser suffers financial loss by incurring expenditure in reliance on negligent professional advice, the client, when spending the money, will often be unaware that that expenditure amounts to loss or damage because of circumstances, existing at the date he or she spends the money, of which the client has no knowledge. A question which the current appeal raises is whether section 11(3) starts the prescriptive clock when the creditor of the obligation is aware that he or she has spent money but does not know that that expenditure will be ineffective."*

In answering that question, the court examined again the interrelation between Section 11(1) and Section 11(3). The issue was what a creditor actually required knowledge of in order for Section 11(3) to operate. The court's conclusion was as follows:-

> *"[20] Section 11(3), which postpones the start of the prescriptive period, is concerned with the awareness of the creditor. But that which the creditor must actually or constructively be aware of before the prescriptive period begins is the same "loss, injury or damage" of which section 11(1) speaks, because subsection (3) uses the same language and also refers back to subsection (1) when it speaks of "loss, injury or damage caused as aforesaid". The phrase "loss, injury or damage" must have the same meaning in each of the subsections of section 11. There is therefore no scope for reading any additional meaning into those words in subsection (3).*
>
> *[21] It follows that section 11(3) does not postpone the start of the prescriptive period until a creditor of an obligation is aware actually or constructively that he or she has suffered a detriment in the sense that something has gone awry rendering the creditor poorer or otherwise at a disadvantage. The creditor does not have to know that he or she has a head of loss. It is sufficient that a creditor is aware that he or she has not obtained something which the creditor had sought or that he or she has incurred expenditure."*

Objectively, this is a very wide interpretation. On the face of it, it would mean that any expenditure incurred by a claimant might cause the prescriptive period to run, even if the claimant is unaware that the expenditure was a "loss", much less that they were aware of a claim in relation to it. That this may operate unfairly in many cases was indeed recognised by the court:-

> "*This approach is harsh on the creditor of the obligation, where the creditor has incurred expenditure which turns out to be wasted or fails to achieve its purpose, because the circumstances when the prescriptive period begins may not prompt an enquiry into the existence or likelihood of such loss. Thus a person may begin a legal action and incur expenditure on legal fees on the basis of negligent legal advice or he or she may purchase a house at an over-value as a result of the negligent advice of a surveyor. In each case the person may be aware of the expenditure but not that it entails the loss. But it offers certainty, at least with the benefit of hindsight. The trustees' formulation by contrast would create uncertainty. If it were necessary in order for the prescriptive period to begin that the creditor be aware that something had gone awry and that he or she has suffered a detriment in the form of wasted expenditure, would an adverse judgment at first instance be sufficient to establish such an awareness of detriment if there were strong grounds for an appeal? The result might be prolonged uncertainty. Further, a requirement that there be an awareness of a head of loss would involve knowledge of the factual cause of the loss, which is an interpretation that this court has rejected in* Morrison v ICL."

Notwithstanding the potential for unfair results, therefore, the court went with legal certainty. It was recognised by the Court that the Scottish Law Commission were looking at this area again in light of *Morrison* and that the law might yet change.

The Current Position

That the law has changed utterly from the *Greater Glasgow Health Board* approach is a fact demonstrated in subsequent case law. It is now well established that knowledge of loss and damage – whether or not one is aware that it is in fact loss or damage, and regardless of whether one is aware that it was caused by negligence – is sufficient to prevent the operation of section 11(3) of the 1973 Act.

In *Anderson -v- Wilson,*[12] for example, it was held that knowledge of the sale of a property on the part of a beneficiary of a deceased's estate operated to bar reliance upon Section 11(3), even where knowledge that the sale had been at undervalue was not gained until 6 years' later.

Similarly, in *Midlothian Council -v- Raeburn Drilling & Geotechnical Limited*[13], the Council raised an action for damages against consulting engineers flowing from advice which the engineers had given in relation to a development of social housing built on former mine workings. The houses were uninhabitable due to the ingress of gasses from the former mine works and ultimately required to be demolished. The Council argued that they were not advised as to the necessity of a gas defence system in relation to the development. It was agreed that the advice was given in 2006. Construction was undertaken between 2007 and 2009. The council were, however, unaware of the issues with gas until 2013. The court held that Section 11(3) did not operate to extend the start of the prescriptive period until 2013. The construction costs incurred between 2007 and 2009 were known to the Council and represented a loss, notwithstanding the Council did not know that it was a loss at the time.

Recent cases have seen an attempt to avoid the operation of Section 11(3) altogether by instead relying upon Section 6(4) (error induced by words or conduct of the debtor). The argument runs that failure of a

---

12 2019 SC 271

13 [2019] CSOH 29

professional to bring a wrongful act to a potential claimant's attention might induce that claimant to refrain from making a claim. At the time of writing there is no decided case on this point, although it has been held that such an argument is relevant and suitable for proof.[14]

Of course, if there is genuinely no knowledge of the loss or damage, and no reasonable diligence would have made the claimant aware, Section 11 still affords a reasonable degree of protection.[15] In such cases the real question will no doubt revolve around what "reasonable diligence" would entail.

In *Virgin Media* it was held that (a) the pursuer could not, with reasonable diligence, have become aware of damage where it did not undertake regular inspections of its equipment; and (b) that whilst knowledge of an agent, guardian or legal representative could be imputed upon a party, knowledge of an independent contractor could not.

Nevertheless, the provision currently operates harshly in most circumstances. The Prescription (Scotland) Act 2018, which is examined in detail below, will make significant changes to the law in this area. Indeed the 2018 Act goes beyond even the *Greater Glasgow Health Board* principle in its reform of the law in this area.

14 *Loretto Housing Association Ltd -v- Cruden Building & Renewals Ltd & others* [2019] CSOH 78

15 See, e.g., *Virgin Media Limited -v- WH Malcolm Limited*, 2018 GWD 36-452

CHAPTER SIX
CONTRACTS GOVERNED BY FOREIGN LAW

The Scottish courts will often be asked to rule on obligations governed by another country's laws. It is very common, for example, for contracts to state that they are to be interpreted in accordance with the laws of England & Wales. Assuming the Scottish courts have jurisdiction, the question can often arise as to what rules on prescription or limitation of actions are to apply to the contract in question.

Section 23A of the 1973 Act deals with the application of private international law to the Scottish rules of prescription.

The general principle is set out in Subsection (1):

> "*Where the substantive law of a country other than Scotland falls to be applied by a Scottish court as the law governing an obligation, the court shall apply any relevant rules of law of that country relating to the extinction of the obligation or the limitation of time within which proceedings may be brought to enforce the obligation to the exclusion of any corresponding rule of Scots law*"

Thus, in an obligation subject to the laws of England & Wales, the six-year limitation period set out in the Limitation Act 1980 would be applied. As with any foreign law pled in a Scottish court, the terms of the relevant rules would be questions of fact, to be proved (if necessary) through the leading of evidence.

There are important derogations from this general rule. First, the Scottish Courts may not apply this rule if doing so would be incompatible with public policy. There does not appear to be any reported authority where this argument has been run.

Second, if the obligation would have prescribed under Scots law prior to the coming into force of the Prescription and Limitation (Scotland) Act 1984 (which introduced this rule), then the rule does not apply. Given the passage of time since the coming into force of the 1984 Act, it is unlikely that many such obligations still subsist.

Finally, Section 23A does not apply to any case where the law of a country other than Scotland falls to be applied by virtue of a choice of law rule contained in the Rome I Regulation[1] or the Rome II Regulation.[2]

This last derogation is a potentially significant one.

In *PRA Group -v- Reilly*[3] the pursuer was the assignee of the original creditor under a regulated consumer credit agreement. The original agreement was said to be governed by the laws of England and Wales and so it was argued that the six-year limitation period applied to the debt.

The defender appears to have originally argued that the Rome I regulation applied, but it was ultimately conceded that it did not due to the age of the contract. That concession having been made, a valiant attempt was made to argue that the Contracts (Applicable Law) Act 1990 applied so that a consumer could not be deprived of the "mandatory rules" of the country of their domicile. Such rules (it was argued) included the Scottish prescription rules. A choice of law clause could not deprive the consumer of the protection of the five-year period and extend time bar to six years.

1 Regulation (EC) No. 593/2008 on the law applicable to contractual obligations

2 Regulation (EC) No. 864/2007 on the law applicable to non-contractual obligations

3 [2018] SC GLA 59

This attempt failed. It was held by the Sheriff that Section 23A provided a complete answer to the question of which rules of time bar applied. The English rules prevailed.

It is of significance, however, that an attempt to invoke the Rome I and Rome II regulations was made. It is unlikely to be the last such attempt, and it begs the question as to whether the court would reach a different view on a contract subject to Rome I or obligation subject to Rome II.

That is untested, but it is suggested that the result is unlikely to have been significantly different, based on the Sheriff's reasoning in *PRA Group*.

Whilst article 6 of Rome I states that a consumer cannot be deprived of protections "which cannot be derogated from by agreement" under the local law (and prescription certainly cannot currently be derogated from by agreement), article 12 makes clear that the applicable law shall govern "the various ways of extinguishing obligations, and prescription and limitation of actions". It would seem difficult to view prescription as a rule which cannot be derogated from where the regulation later specifically sets out that prescription is capable of being governed by the law of the contract.

Even if that is not correct, there is academic comment that an assessment of whether a provision constitutes a protection for the consumer can only be assessed by examining the totality of the protections available in each jurisdiction. If that is correct, it is far from certain that Scots law would override the choice of law in relation to time bar. For one thing, it would have to be established that the local law constituted a "protection" of which the consumer was being deprived. That will not be straightforward, as it would go beyond the question of five versus six years. The foreign limitation period may be longer, but may (for example) run from an earlier date than the Scots rules or may be subject to fewer interruptions, potentially giving the consumer greater protection than Scots law.

In any event, when dealing with claims arising from obligations governed by a foreign law, a prudent practitioner should check carefully which rules apply. If the Rome I and II Regulations do not apply to the obligation, then one can state with some confidence that Section 23A will apply the time bar rules of the foreign jurisdiction. If the foreign rules are likely to be a point of contention they will require to be proven as any other question of fact, and some thought should be given as to the evidence required to support such a claim.

Where Rome I and II Regulations apply, Section 23A specifically does not, and it is to the rules of those regulations to which the practitioner must turn.

CHAPTER SEVEN
LAW REFORM – THE SCOTTISH LAW COMMISSION REPORT, AND PROGRESS THROUGH PARLIAMENT

Rationale for Reform and Approach of the SLC

In the lead judgment in *Morrison -v- ICL Plastics*, referring to the dissenting opinion of Lord Hodge, Lord Reed formed the opinion that the interpretation that he favoured could be a matter for law reform:

> *"Lord Hodge and Lord Toulson, while agreeing with Lord Clyde that sec 11(3) requires the creditor to be aware that loss was 'caused as aforesaid', depart from Lord Clyde's approach by not relating those words back to the words 'caused by an act, neglect or default' in sec 11(1). Instead, they interpret the words 'caused as aforesaid' as meaning 'caused by an act or omission', without any implication that the act or omission is actionable. They suggest that this approach is consistent with the policy of the provision.*
>
> *[31] This approach seems to me to be one which might be recommended for adoption as a matter of law reform: indeed, recommendations to that effect were included among those made by the Scottish Law Commission in its report on Prescription and Limitation of Actions (Latent Damage and Other Related Issues) (no 122) (paras 2.36, 2.55). Those recommendations have not however been implemented by Parliament. It is not possible in my opinion for this court to reach the same result by interpretation of the words used in sec 11(3)"*[1]

1 2014 SC (UKSC) 222, at p.231

In fact the Scottish Law Commission (SLC) have had a long interest in the area of prescription, beginning with the publication of their report in 1970 which led to the 1973 Act.

In their Ninth Programme of Law Reform in 2015, the SLC decided to look again at this area in light in particular of the decision in *Morrison*.

A discussion paper was published in 2016 with some further consultation taking place in March 2017. The SLC's final report was then published in July 2017. By the SLC's own admission, the Report was intended merely to address some of the issues which had arisen over 40 years of judicial scrutiny of the 1973 Act, many of which are set out above.

Put shortly, those issues were:

- The scope of the five-year and 20-year prescriptive periods, and how those periods interplay with statutory provisions in certain areas;
- The discoverability test – i.e. the state of knowledge which a creditor must have before the time period starts to run under Section 11, particularly in light of *Morrison*;
- The "long-stop" prescriptive period, and whether it ought to be possible to interrupt the 20-year period, as it currently is under Section 7;
- Whether the prescriptive period can be or ought to be capable of being contracted out of;
- The burden of proof in establishing whether a claim has prescribed;

- The effect of fraud, concealment and error in the computation of the prescriptive period; and
- The definition of a "relevant claim" for the purposes of determining when the prescriptive period has been interrupted.

Scope of Five-Year and 20-Year Prescriptive Periods and Their Relationship With Statute

As has already been seen most claims and obligations will be subject to one of the prescriptive periods within the 1973 Act, however a number of statutes specify different time limits for bringing claims from those mentioned in the Prescription & Limitation (Scotland) Act 1973. A one-year limit applies to claims for loss and damage to goods carried at sea, for example, and other limits apply to breaches of planning control, copyright or performing rights.

The SLC recognised that this can lead to confusion, as the 1973 Act does not state whether it is to apply where another enactment sets out a different time limit. This can lead to questions as to which statutory provision is to prevail.

The SLC recommended[2] that the question should be put beyond doubt, and that the 1973 Act should not apply where another enactment specifies a different time limit in relation to a particular kind of claim.

On the converse side, where the statute is silent as to the prescriptive period which applies, the SLC recommended that all such statutory obligations should be covered by the five-year prescriptive period unless expressly excluded, and suggest that exclusions should include taxes and duties, child support, and council tax or non-domestic rates.

2 Scot Law Com No 247, para 2.14, Recommendation 1

Finally, the SLC recommended adding to the list of grounds of claim which are covered by the five-year period in order to put certain claims beyond doubt. In particular they recommend including liability arising from pre-contractual negotiations and any obligation relating to the validity of a contract.

The Discoverability Test

The effect of the Supreme Court's judgment in *Morrison* has already been noted. The discoverability test was therefore a major focus for the SLC in their report.

Following *Morrison*, it is now only necessary that the claimant knows that they have suffered loss injury or damage for the clock to start running. Subsequent cases clarified that this was the case even where it is not clear that the loss injury or damage is indeed a loss at the time that it happens.[3]

The SLC report recommends[4] replacing the current test with a formulation whereby the prescriptive period begins to run from the date that a claimant became aware as a matter of fact that:

(a) they had incurred loss injury or damage;

(b) the loss injury or damage was caused by a person's act or omission; and

(c) the identity of that person.

The addition of the third limb is highly significant. In cases where a negligent act was undertaken by a complex corporate structure or under various layers of contract and sub-contract it can take time to determine

3 See *Gordon's Trustees –v- Campbell Riddell Breeze Paterson,* 2017 SLT 1287, together with subsequent cases discussed above.

4 Scot Law Com No. 247, para 3.21, recommendation 6

who was at fault. This provision may therefore extend the time limits considerably.

By way of example, in many cases loss and damage has been caused by works carried out decades earlier. Often the contractors involved have been dissolved, amalgamated, or been struck off the register. Identifying the negligent party can be exceptionally difficult. Taking the time to fully investigate who is at fault is to be welcomed, albeit it begins to tip the balance discussed at the outset of this book in favour of the creditor.

The SLC recognised the difficulties inherent in a very wide provision, and tempered their recommendation by inserting a proviso making clear that actual knowledge that any act or omission is or is not actionable should be irrelevant. In other words the party's knowledge of the *law* is not a relevant consideration. It is their knowledge of the *act* which is relevant.

The SLC also rejected the suggestion that the time limit should only start to run where the loss injury or damage was "material", thus meaning that even knowledge of a trivial loss can start the prescriptive period running. Again, this might be important in a situation such as *Gordon's Trustees*, where the "loss" in question started with a relatively modest incursion of legal fees.

The SLC recommended no change to the existing "reasonable diligence" test whereby the period runs from the time when a claimant was aware or could "with reasonable diligence" have become aware of the fact that they had suffered loss.

Long-Stop Dates

At present, there is a long stop period of 20-years, and it has been seen that the 1973 Act provides that the 20-year prescriptive period is to apply *inter alia* to obligations subject to the five-year period in order to give effect to its "long stop" status. However the 20-year period usually begins to run from the same date as the five-year period, and in many cases it is subject to the same interruptions (relevant acknowledgement or performance towards the obligation). The SLC consulted on whether 20-years should be a true long stop, with no or limited means of extending that period further.

The SLC recommended that the long negative prescription should not be susceptible to interruption in the same way as the five-year period. In the majority of cases, therefore the absolute limit for bringing a successful claim would be 20 years.

This means, of course, that constant extending of the 5-year prescriptive period will eventually hit this limit. Whilst that is not a common situation in practice, it can readily be seen that it might operate unfairly in certain cases.

Contracting Out of the Prescriptive Period

Contractual arrangements seeking to extend or shorten the prescriptive period are currently ineffective, albeit the SLC point out that the statutory provision in this regard could usefully have been clarified.

As the law currently stands, the only ways to extend the prescriptive period at present are either to make a relevant claim (usually by raising court proceedings) or by having the debtor make a "relevant acknowledgment", such as payment towards a debt or a written acknowledgement that the debt exists. In both cases this would start the five-year period over again from that date.

It is not uncommon in England & Wales for parties to enter "standstill agreements" whereby it is formally agreed that the limitation periods will not run for a specified period of time. There are a number of reasons why such agreements are desirable – it allows, for example, some breathing space for discussions or for investigation of a claim or defence.

The SLC recommended that the law of Scotland be changed in order to allow extension of the five-year period through agreement between the parties. Such an extension would be for no more than one year, and the period could only be extended on one occasion. Extension would only be competent where the prescriptive period had started to run but had not yet come to an end. Once at an end, of course, the obligation is extinguished and therefore there would be nothing to extend.

The SLC did not, however, recommend that agreements to disapply or shorten the prescriptive period should have effect, and so the law in this regard would remain unchanged

Burden of Proof

At present the 1973 Act does not stipulate who must prove that a claim or debt has prescribed. It is generally thought that, where prescription is raised, the burden rests with the party seeking to establish the claim to show that it has not prescribed.

In *Pelagic Freezing (Scotland) Ltd –v- Lovie Construction Ltd*,[5] and more recently in *Macdonald –v- Clydesdale Bank plc*[6] this was clearly held to be the case. However, there are conflicting authorities. The case of *Alton B Copland Limited*[7] is an example where Lord Hodge appear to have taken the view that the defender had "failed to demonstrate" that the obligation to make payment was enforceable more than five years prior to proceedings being raised, which suggests that he considered the onus to be on them to do so.

The SLC recommended putting this beyond doubt and enshrining it within the legislation such that it would be for the party asserting a claim to prove that it has not prescribed.

5 [2010] CSOH 145

6 [2017] SC EDIN 65

7 [2010] CSOH 135

Fraud, Concealment and Error

As has been seen, the law disregards "any period during which, by reason of (i) fraud on the part of the debtor or any person acting on his behalf, or (ii) error induced by words or conduct of the debtor... the creditor was induced to refrain from making a relevant claim" in the computation of the prescriptive period.

There was conflicting authority on the question of the extent to which the debtor's words or actions must have knowingly induced the claimant not to act, nor the extent to which a creditor must have known that they had a claim but been induced not to pursue it.

The report came out before the judgment in *Heather Capital*, which is discussed above and makes it clear that "error" or "inducement" has a particularly wide interpretation and applies regardless of whether the conduct is active, passive, knowing or unknowing.

As it happens the SLC's conclusion matches the outcome of *Heather Capital.* The SLC recommend that the matter be enshrined in legislation such that the five-year prescriptive period shall be suspended in relation to any creditor who has been caused by the debtor, innocently or otherwise, not to raise proceedings.

In light of *Heather Capital* this does not effectively change the position in law, but does put it beyond doubt by giving the *Heather Capital* principle a statutory basis.

Relevant Claim

The SLC did not intend to look at the question of a relevant claim, however a number of respondents to the SLC's consultation exercise had raised questions around the definition of a "relevant claim" for the purposes of the interruption of prescription.

In light of those responses, the SLC made a recommendation in relation to the question of when prescription starts to run from again once a "relevant claim" has been made.

The practical issue is this: in the case of court proceedings, the Act might be interpreted as restarting the prescriptive clock either on the date upon which the proceedings are served, or on the date upon which they are finally disposed of.

Whilst most court proceedings are dealt with in a relatively short timescale, some can run for a number of years, and so the question can be important. If the clock re-starts at the point of serving the action, any claim in dependence for greater than five years would be at risk from prescription.

The SLC favoured the latter interpretation and recommended clarifying the law so that the prescriptive period will start to run again only once the relevant claim has been finally disposed of.

Passage of the Bill

These were the primary recommendations of the SLC's report. The report also included a draft Bill enshrining these recommendations primarily by way of amendment to the 1973 Act.

The report found early traction with Scottish Government. In September 2017 the Scottish Government published its Programme for Government for Scotland. In that programme, the Prescription (Scotland) Bill was named as one of 16 Bills which the Government intended to introduce during the 2017/18 term.

The Bill was introduced on 8th February 2018 and was assigned to the Delegated Powers and Law Reform Committee. Evidence was gathered (primarily in writing) and the Bill was further considered by the Committee between February and June 2018, with the stage 1 Debate taking place on 27th June 2018. The Act passed following the Stage 3 Debate on 8th December 2018 and received Royal Assent on 18th December 2018.

At the time of writing the Act is not yet in force. Some reasons for that are explored below.

Parliamentary Scrutiny

The Bill did not pass without significant scrutiny. In particular the proposal to exempt taxes and duties, Council Tax and non-domestic rates, child maintenance and recovery of overpayments of certain benefits and social security payments from the scope of the short negative prescription was considered by the Committee at length.

Views in relation to that provision were varied. One local authority considered that the provision may have unintended consequences.[8] The Law Society of Scotland considered that there was no legal or logical reason for such debts to be treated differently,[9] and that in relation to council tax and non-domestic rates the exemption was "unfair".[10]

As a result, the Committee recommended at Stage 1 that the Government provide further rationale for excepting council tax and business rates from the five-year rule, and undertook to write to all 32 local authorities in Scotland prior to stage 2 in order to determine how often the 20-year prescriptive period required to be relied upon.[11]

In addition to the exemptions to the five-year rule, a number of other issues were raised during Stage 1. These included substantive legal matters, such as the interaction between the new discoverability test and

---

8 *Prescription (Scotland) Bill: Stage 1 Report (SP Paper 354), at para 81*

9 *Ibid*, at para 82

10 *Ibid*, at para 86

11 *Ibid*, at paras 111 to 113.

the principle of joint and several liability.[12] They also included less substantive matters such as the use of certain outmoded language within the Bill (in particular the use of phrases such as "unsoundness of mind", which one witness considered to be "insulting and offensive".[13] The Scottish Government responded to those issues by letter to the Committee in advance of Stage 2.

The issue of council tax and recovery of reserved social security overpayments remained controversial as the Bill entered Stage 3. Amendments were introduced seeking to remove the exemptions for these types of debt, which would have made them subject to the five-year prescriptive period. Those amendments did not pass, however, and the Bill as passed was largely the same as the Bill which was introduced.

---

12 *Ibid*, at paras 164 *et seq.*

13 *Ibid*, at paras 287 *et seq.*

CHAPTER EIGHT
THE PRESCRIPTION (SCOTLAND) ACT 2018

The Act was granted Royal Assent on 18th December 2018. It is not yet in force, however. What follows is an examination of the key elements of the Act as passed. Clearly the interpretation of many of these provisions has not yet been subject to judicial scrutiny, and it is quite possible that judicial examination of the Act will raise anomalies not considered here.

Obligations to Pay Damages and Delictual Obligations

Paragraph 1(d) of Schedule 1 currently provides that the five-year prescriptive period will apply to "any obligation arising from liability… to make reparation". The Scottish Law Commission had recognised that "liability to make reparation" was potentially ambiguous. As a result, the 2018 Act amends this provision so that it reads:-

> *"(d)…any obligation to pay damages (whatever the source of the obligation); [and]*
>
> *(da) …any obligation arising from delict, not being an obligation falling within any other provision of this paragraph"*[1]

The effect of this change is twofold. Firstly an "obligation to pay damages" is considered to be wider in scope than "reparation". The latter was considered to be limited to payment of damages arising from a wrongful act. The new provision makes clear that the source of the obligation to pay damages is not relevant.

---

1 2018 Act, Section 1(2)

Second, the new provision makes clear that claims arising from delict which are not claims for reparation are included within the five-year period. Again, this clarifies the scope of the short negative prescription. Some consequential amendments are made to Section 11 of the 1973 Act to accommodate these changes.

The starting point of the prescriptive period for obligations to pay damages is also slightly amended by the 2018 Act.[2] Where the phrase "act, neglect or default" was previously used in Section 11 of the 1973 Act, this has been changed to "act or omission". In part, this change is intended to underline that the creditors knowledge of the legal position (i.e. whether someone has been negligent or in default of a duty or obligation) is not relevant. Knowledge of the act or omission is sufficient. The SLC also sought consistency with other provisions of the 1973 Act where this formulation is used.

Of most significance in relation to such claims, however, is the overhaul of the discoverability test. This is achieved by inserting a new test into section 11[3] requiring a claimant to have knowledge of three facts:

> *"(a) that loss, injury or damage has occurred,*
>
> *(b) that the loss, injury or damage was caused by a person's act or omission, and*
>
> *(c) the identity of that person"*[4]

The description of the three elements as being "facts" is important. It is knowledge of the factual position which triggers the provision and not knowledge of the legal position. This is underlined by the new Section 11(3B), which states:-

2 2018 Act, Section 5

3 Subsection (3A)

4 Inserted by 2018 Act, Section 5(5)

> *"It does not matter for the purposes of subsections (3) and (3A) whether the creditor is aware that the act or omission that caused the loss, injury or damage is actionable in law"*

Thus the Supreme Court's decision in *Morrison* and the subsequent cases referred to above is reversed.

A final, but important provision in relation to obligations to pay damages is contained in Section 8 of the 2018 Act. It amends Section 11 of the 1973 Act insofar as it applies to the long negative prescription. The current position is that subsections (1) and (2) of Section 11 apply to the long negative prescription, meaning that unless the discoverability test is engaged, the 20-year period will start to run at the same time as the five-year period.

Section 8 amends this so that it is clear that the 20-year period will begin to run on the date that the act or omission occurred, or where the act or omission was a continuing one, the date upon which it ceased.[5] The practical effect of this is that the date of loss, injury or damage is not relevant to the long negative prescription, and instead the date of the act or omission (whether known about or not) will commence the 20-year long stop period.

Prescriptive Periods in Other Statutes

Section 3 of the 2018 Act repeals a number of the outdated provisions of Schedule 1 of the 1973 Act, such as claims for redemption of feuduty, most of which will have long since prescribed.

This section also inserts a new sub-paragraph (h) into paragraph 1 of schedule 1, which states that the five-year period shall apply:

---

5 2018 Act, Section 8, inserting new Section 11(4) into the 1973 Act

"(h) to any obligation to make payment arising under an enactment (whenever passed or made) not being an obligation falling under any other provision of this paragraph"[6]

If a statute is silent in relation to prescription, therefore, this provision applies the five year period. Where a statute does make provision in relation to prescription, however, the 1973 Act will now explicitly recognise those provisions.[7]

As we have seen, however, the 2018 Act then provides for a number of exceptions to this general rule which were not passed without controversy.

These exceptions were:

"(fa) to any obligation to pay taxes or duties that are recoverable by the Crown, or to pay any penalty, interest or other sum that is recoverable as if it were an amount of such taxes or duties;

(fb) to any obligation to pay a sum recoverable under—

(i) Part 3 (overpayments and adjustments of benefit) of the Social Security Administration Act 1992;

(ii) section 127(c) (recovery of income support in certain circumstances) of the Social Security Contributions and Benefits Act 1992; or

(iii) Part 1 (tax credits) of the Tax Credits Act 2002;

(fc) to any obligation to pay child support maintenance under the Child Support Act 1991;

6 2018 Act, Section 3(2)(b), inserting new paragraph 1(h) into schedule 1 of the 1973 Act

7 2018 Act, Section 9, inserting new Section 7A into the 1973 Act

(fd) to any obligation to pay—

(i) council tax under Part 2 of the Local Government Finance Act 1992;

(ii) non-domestic rates levied under section 7B(2) of the Local Government (Scotland) Act 1975; or

(iii) any surcharge, fees, expenses or other sum recoverable in connection with the enforcement of an obligation to pay such council tax or rates"[8]

At the time of debate in the Scottish parliament the Government position in relation to these provisions was that they were intended to maintain the *status quo*, and that the Bill was not the correct place to innovate on the law. Whilst that may leave the door open to further examination of the position in the future, the amendments seeking to remove the provisions were roundly defeated and the Government position appeared sympathetic to councils seeking to recover money to pay for local services. It seems unlikely that anything will change in this regard in the near future, therefore.

A quirk of the new provision is that it disapplies the 20-year period to UK-wide social security and benefit overpayments, but not to those administered by the Scottish Government. During the debate on the Act, the Government indicated that this was due to the interaction between devolved and reserved powers, and it was suggested that the Scottish Government did not have the power to apply the short negative prescription to UK-wide benefits or social security legislation.

8 2018 Act, section 3(3)(b), inserting new sub paragraphs to Schedule 1, paragraph 2 of the 1973 Act

Debtor's Intention

As recommended by the Scottish Law Commission, the 2018 Act clarifies the law such that where a person fails to make a claim due to fraud or error on the part of the debtor, the consciousness or otherwise of that decision is immaterial. As we have seen, this appeared to be the law as it stood in any event, however the matter has now been put beyond doubt.

The 2018 Act makes two changes to Section 6 of the 1973 Act in order to give effect to this. Firstly, the Act removes the confusing concept of "inducement" from the Act, so that a claimant no longer requires to have been "induced to refrain" from making a claim, and now simply requires to "fail to make" a claim.[9] Secondly, the 2018 Act inserts a new subsection 4A into Section 6, which reads:

> *"For the purposes of subsection (4)(a), it does not matter whether the debtor, or the person acting on the debtor's behalf, intended the fraud or the words or conduct to cause the creditor to fail to make a relevant claim"*[10]

The test is no clear and unambiguous. The Scottish Law Commission concluded that this formulation was a more objective test and that it operated in a fairer way than a more restrictive test.[11]

Relevant Claims – Final Disposal

There are three sections of the 2018 Act which concern the concept of a "relevant claim". These deal respectively with (a) what should be considered a relevant claim; (b) how long a relevant claim may run for, and (c) when such a claim might be considered definitively disposed of.

9 2018 Act, Section 4(2), altering the wording of Section 6(4) of the 1973 Act

10 2018 Act, Section 4(3)

11 See Scot Law Com Report No. 247, para 7.10

In relation to the first aspect, it had been identified by the SLC that there appeared to be obvious omissions from the definition of what might be a relevant claim.[12] In particular a relevant claim might be made by way of a claim in certain insolvency processes, but not others.

Section 10 of the 2018 Act deals with this aspect, adding to the definitions of a relevant claim found in Section 9 and 22A of the 1973. Under the new provision, an appointment or application to appoint an administrator or receiver under the Insolvency Act 1986 will constitute a relevant claim. The submission of a claim to an administrator or receiver would likewise constitute a relevant claim.

Section 11 of the 2018 Act deals with an issue which was not raised in the SLC's discussion paper, but which the SLC identified as a result of consultation. The issue concerns the nature of a relevant claim in court proceedings and whether the interruption occurs upon the service of the proceedings, or whether the interruption continues until the claim is finally disposed of. Section 11(2) of the 2018 Act clarifies this issue by inserting new wording into Section 9 of the 1973 Act. This wording reads:

> *"Where a relevant claim is made in relation to an obligation to which section 6 or 8A applies, the claim is to be treated for the purposes of that section as being made continuously until the claim is finally disposed of"*[13]

It is accordingly now clear that the interruption of the prescriptive period continues until final disposal of the court proceedings.

This does, however, then lead to a question of what constitutes "final disposal" for these purposes. Section 12 of the 2018 Act deals with that question. There are four scenarios mentioned, which confirm that a claim is finally disposed of:-

12 Scot Law Com Report No. 247, paras 7.16 to 7.18

13 New Section 9(2A) of the 1973 Act

"(a) when a decision disposing of the claim is made, if there is no right of appeal against the decision,

(b) if there is a right of appeal with leave or permission against such a decision—

(i) when the time period for seeking leave or permission to appeal has expired without an application for leave or permission having been made, or

(ii) when leave or permission to appeal is refused,

(c) if leave or permission to appeal against such a decision has been granted or is not required, when the time period for making an appeal has expired without an appeal having been made, or

(d) when the claim is withdrawn or abandoned"[14]

It is further clarified in the Act that "a decision disposing of the claim" includes a decision in an appeal against an earlier decision.

Burden of Proof

As has already been seen, there is some uncertainty in the law as to where the burden of proof lies in a case where prescription is raised as a defence. The prevailing view appears to be that the onus rests with the person seeking to prove that a claim has *not* prescribed, however we have seen some deviation from this rule in practice.

Section 14 of the 2018 Act inserts a new Section 13A into the 1973 Act which is intended to put the question beyond doubt.

In terms of that section, where a question arises as to whether an obligation or right has prescribed, a presumption will now arise that it has prescribed unless the contrary is proved by the creditor. The onus of

14 2018 Act, section 12, inserting new Section 9A into the 1973 Act

proof therefore falls squarely upon the creditor, who is usually the pursuer in an action.

The 2018 Act also adds a new Section 22A(7A), extending this rule to claims under Part I of the Consumer Protection Act 1987.

Long-Stop Dates

As set out above, an area of concern for the SLC was that the 20-year period was intended to be a long-stop date after which the vast majority of rights and obligations would expire. Instead, the 1973 Act provided that the long negative prescription could be interrupted in much the same way as the short negative prescription. That led to the prospect of claims and rights essentially becoming imprescriptible due to continued interruption.

A secondary issue was that the 20-year period generally ran from the same date as the five-year period and so the start of the period could, in certain circumstances, be delayed considerably.

Section 6 of the 2018 Act deals with these concerns.

In the first place the starting point from which the 20-year period runs is amended. It will no longer be interrupted by a relevant claim being made or through a relevant acknowledgment, and will simply run for 20 years from the date upon which the obligation becomes enforceable.[15]

As recommended by the SLC, this has been tempered to a degree by the insertion of new provisions into the 1973 Act[16] which make clear that where a relevant claim is made prior to the end of the prescriptive period the period will not expire until the claim is finally disposed of or

15 2018 Act, Section 6, amending section 7 of the 1973 Act

16 Section 7(3) to (5)

otherwise comes to an end. This allows for claims which would otherwise prescribe during the currency of the claim to survive until a final disposal is made. In the case of successful court proceedings that will usually result in a decree. The obligation to obtemper a court decree is itself subject to the 20-year period, as we have seen above.

The position is broadly the same in relation to property rights under section 8 of the 1973 Act.

"Standstill" Agreements

The final element introduced by the 2018 Act concerns Section 13 of the 1973 Act. As it currently stands, that section states that any agreement purporting to provide that a right or obligation subject to prescription shall not have effect "shall be null".

The SLC identified a number of issues with this provision. Whilst it clearly appears to prevent a lengthening of the prescriptive period, for example, it is not so clear whether it applies to an agreement shortening the period.[17] The SLC also queried whether it would be desirable to introduce a so-called "standstill agreement" into the law of Scotland, and in what circumstances. Such agreements are common in other jurisdictions, most notably in England & Wales.

Ultimately the 2018 Act replaced Section 13. Instead of a prohibition on contracting out, the provision is now titled "restrictions on contracting out". It provides for the creditor and debtor to an obligation to extend the prescriptive period.[18] This only applies to prescriptive periods under Section 6 (short negative prescription) and 8A (contributions between wrongdoers), and cannot therefore be used to extend the long negative prescription.

---

17 Scot Law Com, Discussion Paper No 160, at para 7.3(3); see also *Ferguson -v- McIntyre* 1993 SLT 1269

18 1973 Act, Section 13(1), to be inserted by 2018 Act, Section 13

Such an agreement may only be entered into after the period in question has commenced, and before it would otherwise expire.[19] It may only be entered into once in relation to an obligation and may not extend the period for more than one year.[20]

The new provision does not allow the disapplication or alteration of a prescriptive period other than in accordance with such an agreement. The wording of the new section therefore clarifies that a shortening of the prescriptive period is to be of no effect.[21]

The intended effect of the section is to allow parties to negotiate or investigate matters whilst maintaining the status quo. In their report[22] the SLC hoped that this would reduce the need for "protective" court proceedings to be raised in order to preserve a party's position.

Transitional Arrangements and Coming Into Force

At the time of writing the 2018 Act is not in force, and there is no date currently set for the coming into force of the Act.

Clearly the transitional arrangements will require careful consideration. For example, if the changes to the discoverability test were to be introduced retrospectively, it may result in claims which had prescribed under the current law being revived. Likewise claims where prescription has started to run under the current regime would not commence until later under the new one. A good deal of thought will require to be given to precisely where the cut-off lies in order to ensure that fairness is maintained.

---

19 *Ibid*, new section 13(2)(a)

20 *Ibid*, new section 13(2)(b) and (c)

21 *Ibid*, new Section 13(4)

22 Scot Law Com No 247, at paras 5.4 and 5.5

It is not anticipated that the 2018 Act will come into force until at least mid-2020.

MORE BOOKS BY LAW BRIEF PUBLISHING

A selection of our other titles available now:-

'Ellis on Credit Hire – Sixth Edition' by Aidan Ellis & Tim Kevan
'A Practical Guide to Coercive Control for Legal Practitioners and Victims' by Rachel Horman
'A Practical Guide to Rights Over Airspace and Subsoil' by Daniel Gatty
'Tackling Disclosure in the Criminal Courts – A Practitioner's Guide' by Narita Bahra QC & Don Ramble
'A Practical Guide to the Law of Driverless Cars – Second Edition' by Alex Glassbrook, Emma Northey & Scarlett Milligan
'A Practical Guide to TOLATA Claims' by Greg Williams
'Artificial Intelligence – The Practical Legal Issues' by John Buyers
'A Practical Guide to the Law of Bullying and Harassment in the Workplace' by Philip Hyland
'How to Be a Freelance Solicitor: A Practical Guide to the SRA-Regulated Freelance Solicitor Model' by Paul Bennett
'A Practical Guide to Prison Injury Claims' by Malcolm Johnson
'A Practical Guide to the Small Claims Track' by Dominic Bright
'A Practical Guide to Advising Clients at the Police Station' by Colin Stephen McKeown-Beaumont
'A Practical Guide to Antisocial Behaviour Injunctions' by Iain Wightwick
'Practical Mediation: A Guide for Mediators, Advocates, Advisers, Lawyers, and Students in Civil, Commercial, Business, Property, Workplace, and Employment Cases' by Jonathan Dingle with John Sephton
'The Mini-Pupillage Workbook' by David Boyle
'Planning Obligations Demystified: A Practical Guide to Planning Obligations and Section 106 Agreements' by Bob Mc Geady & Meyric Lewis
'A Practical Guide to Crofting Law' by Brian Inkster

'A Practical Guide to Spousal Maintenance' by Liz Cowell
'A Practical Guide to the Law of Domain Names and Cybersquatting' by Andrew Clemson
'A Practical Guide to the Law of Gender Pay Gap Reporting' by Harini Iyengar
'A Practical Guide to the Rights of Grandparents in Children Proceedings' by Stuart Barlow
'NHS Whistleblowing and the Law' by Joseph England
'Employment Law and the Gig Economy' by Nigel Mackay & Annie Powell
'A Practical Guide to the General Data Protection Regulation (GDPR)' by Keith Markham
'A Practical Guide to Noise Induced Hearing Loss (NIHL) Claims' by Andrew Mckie, Ian Skeate, Gareth McAloon
'An Introduction to Beauty Negligence Claims – A Practical Guide for the Personal Injury Practitioner' by Greg Almond
'Intercompany Agreements for Transfer Pricing Compliance' by Paul Sutton
'Zen and the Art of Mediation' by Martin Plowman
'A Practical Guide to the SRA Principles, Individual and Law Firm Codes of Conduct 2019 – What Every Law Firm Needs to Know' by Paul Bennett
'A Practical Guide to Licensing Law for Commercial Property Lawyers' by Niall McCann & Richard Williams
'A Practical Guide to Adoption for Family Lawyers' by Graham Pegg
'A Practical Guide to Industrial Disease Claims' by Andrew Mckie & Ian Skeate
'A Practical Guide to Redundancy' by Philip Hyland
'A Practical Guide to Vicarious Liability' by Mariel Irvine
'A Practical Guide to Claims Arising from Delays in Diagnosing Cancer' by Bella Webb
'A Practical Guide to Applications for Landlord's Consent and Variation of Leases' by Mark Shelton
'A Practical Guide to Relief from Sanctions Post-Mitchell and Denton' by Peter Causton
'A Practical Guide to Equity Release for Advisors' by Paul Sams
'A Practical Guide to Unlawful Eviction and Harassment' by Stephanie Lovegrove

'A Practical Guide to the Law Relating to Food' by Ian Thomas
'A Practical Guide to the Ending of Assured Shorthold Tenancies' by Elizabeth Dwomoh
'A Practical Guide to Financial Services Claims' by Chris Hegarty
'The Law of Houses in Multiple Occupation: A Practical Guide to HMO Proceedings' by Julian Hunt
'A Practical Guide to Unlawful Eviction and Harassment' by Stephanie Lovegrove
'A Practical Guide to Solicitor and Client Costs' by Robin Dunne
'A Practical Guide to Wrongful Conception, Wrongful Birth and Wrongful Life Claims' by Rebecca Greenstreet
'Occupiers, Highways and Defective Premises Claims: A Practical Guide Post-Jackson – 2nd Edition' by Andrew Mckie
'A Practical Guide to Financial Ombudsman Service Claims' by Adam Temple & Robert Scrivenor
'A Practical Guide to the Law of Enfranchisement and Lease Extension' by Paul Sams
'A Practical Guide to Marketing for Lawyers – 2nd Edition' by Catherine Bailey & Jennet Ingram
'A Practical Guide to Advising Schools on Employment Law' by Jonathan Holden
'Certificates of Lawful Use and Development: A Guide to Making and Determining Applications' by Bob Mc Geady & Meyric Lewis
'A Guide to Consent in Clinical Negligence Post-Montgomery' by Lauren Sutherland QC
'A Practical Guide to Running Housing Disrepair and Cavity Wall Claims: 2nd Edition' by Andrew Mckie & Ian Skeate
'A Practical Guide to Holiday Sickness Claims – 2nd Edition' by Andrew Mckie & Ian Skeate
'Arguments and Tactics for Personal Injury and Clinical Negligence Claims' by Dorian Williams
'A Practical Guide to QOCS and Fundamental Dishonesty' by James Bentley
'A Practical Guide to Drone Law' by Rufus Ballaster, Andrew Firman, Eleanor Clot
'A Practical Guide to Compliance for Personal Injury Firms Working With Claims Management Companies' by Paul Bennett

'A Practical Guide to the Landlord and Tenant Act 1954: Commercial Tenancies' by Richard Hayes & David Sawtell
'A Practical Guide to Dog Law for Owners and Others' by Andrea Pitt
'RTA Allegations of Fraud in a Post-Jackson Era: The Handbook – 2nd Edition' by Andrew Mckie
'RTA Personal Injury Claims: A Practical Guide Post-Jackson' by Andrew Mckie
'On Experts: CPR35 for Lawyers and Experts' by David Boyle
'An Introduction to Personal Injury Law' by David Boyle
'A Practical Guide to Claims Arising From Accidents Abroad and Travel Claims' by Andrew Mckie & Ian Skeate
'A Practical Guide to Chronic Pain Claims' by Pankaj Madan
'A Practical Guide to Claims Arising from Fatal Accidents' by James Patience
'A Practical Approach to Clinical Negligence Post-Jackson' by Geoffrey Simpson-Scott
'Employers' Liability Claims: A Practical Guide Post-Jackson' by Andrew Mckie
'A Practical Guide to Subtle Brain Injury Claims' by Pankaj Madan
'A Practical Guide to Costs in Personal Injury Cases' by Matthew Hoe
'The No Nonsense Solicitors' Practice: A Guide To Running Your Firm' by Bettina Brueggemann
'The Queen's Counsel Lawyer's Omnibus: 20 Years of Cartoons from The Times 1993-2013' by Alex Steuart Williams

www.ingramcontent.com/pod-product-compliance
Lightning Source LLC
LaVergne TN
LVHW022109200926
848481LV00003B/1114